Communications in Computer and Information Science 1607

More information about this series at https://link.springer.com/bookseries/7899

Donald Ferguson · Markus Helfert ·
Claus Pahl (Eds.)

Cloud Computing
and Services Science

11th International Conference, CLOSER 2021
Virtual Event, April 28–30, 2021
Revised Selected Papers

Editors
Donald Ferguson
Columbia University
New York, NY, USA

Markus Helfert
Maynooth University
Maynooth, Kildare, Ireland

Claus Pahl 🅙
Free University of Bozen-Bolzano
Bolzano, Bolzano, Italy

ISSN 1865-0929   ISSN 1865-0937 (electronic)
Communications in Computer and Information Science
ISBN 978-3-031-21636-7   ISBN 978-3-031-21637-4 (eBook)
https://doi.org/10.1007/978-3-031-21637-4

This Springer imprint is published by the registered company Springer Nature Switzerland AG
The registered company address is: Gewerbestrasse 11, 6330 Cham, Switzerland

Preface

The present book includes extended and revised versions of a set of selected papers from the 11th International Conference on cloud computing and services science (CLOSER 2021), held during April 28–30, 2021, as a web-based event due to the COVID-19 pandemic.

CLOSER 2021 received 51 paper submissions from 20 countries, of which 10% were included in this book. The papers were selected by the event chairs and their selection is based on a number of criteria that include the classifications and comments provided by the Program Committee members, the session chairs' assessment, and also the program chairs' global view of all papers included in the technical program. The authors of selected papers were then invited to submit a revised and extended version of their paper having at least 30% innovative material.

The 11th International Conference on cloud computing and services science, CLOSER 2021, focused on the highly important area of cloud computing, inspired by some recent advances that concern the infrastructure, operations, and available services through the global network. Further, the conference considered the essential the link to services science, acknowledging the service-orientation in most current IT-driven collaborations. The conference is nevertheless not about the union of these two (already broad) fields, but about cloud computing where we are also interested in how services science can provide theory, methods, and techniques to design, analyze, manage, market, and study various aspects of cloud computing.

The papers selected to be included in this book contribute to the understanding of relevant trends of current research on cloud computing and services science. The selected papers demonstrate the relevance of the cloud computing paradigm for research and practice alike, which now even extends into a continuum including Edge and IoT concerns. In the core cloud technology space, the deployment of services remains an active area. Also, security is an ongoing research focus for service management and operation in cloud environments. Of increasing importance are artificial intelligence approaches to data and service management across the whole cloud continuum.

We would like to thank all the authors for their contributions and also the reviewers who helped ensure the quality of this publication.

April 2021

Donald Ferguson
Markus Helfert
Claus Pahl

Organization

Conference Chair

Claus Pahl   Free University of Bozen-Bolzano, Italy

Program Co-chairs

Markus Helfert   Maynooth University, Ireland
Donald Ferguson   Columbia University, USA

Program Committee

Luca Abeni   Scuola Superiore Sant'Anna, Italy
Claudio Ardagna   Universita degli Studi di Milano, Italy
Simona Bernardi   Universidad de Zaragoza, Spain
Luiz F. Bittencourt   UNICAMP, Brazil
Andrey Brito   Universidade Federal de Campina Grande, Brazil
Claudia Canali   University of Modena and Reggio Emilia, Italy
Manuel Capel-Tuñón   University of Granada, Spain
Eddy Caron   École normale supérieure de Lyon, France
John Cartlidge   University of Bristol, UK
Anis Charfi   Carnegie Mellon University, Qatar
Richard Chbeir   Université de Pau et des Pays de l'Adour (UPPA),
                                           France
Augusto Ciuffoletti   Università di Pisa, Italy
Daniela Claro   Universidade Federal da Bahia (UFBA), Brazil
Thierry Coupaye   Orange, France
Sabrina De Capitani di Vimercati   Università degli Studi di Milano, Italy
Giuseppe Di Modica   University of Catania, Italy
Vincent Emeakaroha   Munster Technological University, Ireland
Massimo Ficco   University of Campania Luigi Vanvitelli, Italy
Somchart Fugkeaw   Thammasat University, Thailand
Fabrizio Gagliardi   Barcelona Supercomputing Centre, Spain
Vinicius Garcia   Federal University of Pernambuco, Brazil
Antonio García Loureiro   University of Santiago de Compostela, Spain
Francisco García-Sánchez   University of Murcia, Spain
Sukhpal Gill   Queen Mary University of London, UK
Lee Gillam   University of Surrey, UK

Antonios Gouglidis   Lancaster University, UK
Nils Gruschka   University of Oslo, Norway
Franz Hauck   Ulm University, Germany
Ilian Ilkov   IBM Nederland B.V., Netherlands
Anca Ionita   Politehnica University of Bucharest, Romania
Ivan Ivanov   SUNY Empire State College, USA
Martin Jaatun   University of Stavanger, Norway
Keith Jeffery   Independent Consultant (previously Science and
                                    Technology Facilities Council), UK

Meiko Jensen   Kiel University of Applied Sciences, Germany
Ming Jiang   University of Sunderland, UK
Carlos Juiz   Universitat de les Illes Balears, Spain
Attila Kertesz   University of Szeged, Hungary
Hamzeh Khazaei   York University, Canada
Maria Kihl   Lund University, Sweden
Carsten Kleiner   University of Applied Sciences and Arts
                                    Hannover, Germany

George Kousiouris   Harokopio University of Athens, Greece
József Kovács   MTA SZTAKI, Hungary
Nane Kratzke   Lübeck University of Applied Sciences, Germany
Adam Krechowicz   Kielce University of Technology, Poland
Riccardo Lancellotti   University of Modena and Reggio Emilia, Italy
Frank Leymann   University of Stuttgart, Germany
Shijun Liu   Shandong University, China
Xiaodong Liu   Edinburgh Napier University, UK
Francesco Longo   Università degli Studi di Messina, Italy
Joseph Loyall   BBN Technologies, USA
Mauro Marinoni   Scuola Superiore Sant'Anna of Pisa, Italy
Ioannis Mavridis   University of Macedonia, Greece
Andreas Menychtas   BioAssist S.A., Greece
Kamran Munir   University of the West of England, UK
Hidemoto Nakada   National Institute of Advanced Industrial Science
                                    and Technology (AIST), Japan

Philippe Navaux   Federal University of Rio Grande Do Sul, Brazil
Stephan Olariu   Old Dominion University, USA
Tolga Ovatman   Istanbul Technical University, Turkey
Michael Palis   Rutgers University, USA
David Paul   University of New England, Australia
Dana Petcu   West University of Timisoara, Romania
Laurent Philippe   Université de Franche-Comté, France
Agostino Poggi   University of Parma, Italy
Antonio Puliafito   Università degli Studi di Messina, Italy

Manuel Ramos-Cabrer	University of Vigo, Spain
Christoph Reich	Furtwangen University, Germany
Pedro Rosa	Federal University of Uberlandia, Brazil
António Rosado da Cruz	Instituto Politécnico de Viana do Castelo, Portugal
Belen Ruiz-Mezcua	Carlos III University of Madrid, Spain
Elena Sanchez-Nielsen	Universidad de La Laguna, Spain
Patrizia Scandurra	University of Bergamo, Italy
Erich Schikuta	Universität Wien, Austria
Wael Sellami	University of Sfax, Tunisia
Richard Sinnott	University of Melbourne, Australia
Frank Siqueira	Federal University of Santa Catarina, Brazil
Ellis Solaiman	Newcastle University, UK
Jacopo Soldani	Università di Pisa, Italy
Josef Spillner	Zurich University of Applied Sciences, Switzerland
Marc St-Hilaire	Carleton University, Canada
Yasuyuki Tahara	University of Electro-Communications, Japan
Cedric Tedeschi	IRISA - University of Rennes 1, France
Gilbert Tekli	Nobatek, France
Guy Tel-Zur	Ben-Gurion University of the Negev (BGU), Israel
Orazio Tomarchio	University of Catania, Italy
Slim Trabelsi	SAP, France
Tullio Vardanega	University of Padua, Italy
Yiannis Verginadis	National Technical University of Athens, Greece
Tomáš Vitvar	Oracle and Czech Technical University in Prague, Czech Republic
Karoline Wild	University of Stuttgart, Germany
Michael Zapf	Georg Simon Ohm University of Applied Sciences, Germany
Chrysostomos Zeginis	ICS-FORTH, Greece

Additional Reviewers

Sabri Allani	Université de Pau et des Pays de l'Adour (UPPA), France
Hamza Baniata	University of Szeged, Hungary
Zakaria Benomar	University of Messina, Italy
Belen Bermejo	University of the Balearic Islands, Spain
Athanasios Dimitriadis	University of Macedonia, Greece
Stephen Fan	Univeristy of Alberta, Canada
Kálmán Képes	University of Stuttgart, Germany
Changyuan Lin	Univeristy of Alberta, Canada

Nima Mahmoudi   Univeristy of Alberta, Canada
Andras Markus   University of Szeged, Hungary
Adel Noureddine   Université de Pau et des Pays de l'Adour (UPPA),
                             France
Tamas Pflanzner   University of Szeged, Hungary
Nachiket Tapas   University of Messina, Italy
Nikolaos Tsinganos   University of Macedonia, Greece

Invited Speakers

Maarten van Steen   University of Twente, Netherlands
Ingo Weber   TU Berlin, Germany
Ivica Crnkovic   Chalmers University of Technology, Sweden
Samuel Kounev   University of Würzburg, Germany

Contents

Tailoring Technology-Agnostic Deployment Models to Production-Ready Deployment Technologies

Jacopo Soldani[1]([⊠]), Uwe Breitenbücher[2], Antonio Brogi[1], Leonardo Frioli[1], Frank Leymann[2], and Michael Wurster[2]

[1] Department of Computer Science, University of Pisa, Pisa, Italy
jacopo.soldani@unipi.it
[2] Institute of Architecture of Application Systems, University of Stuttgart, Stuttgart, Germany

Abstract. Most of existing production-ready deployment automation technologies enable declaratively specifying the target deployment for a multi-service application, which can then be automatically enforced. Each technology however relies on a different deployment modelling language, hence hampering the portability of an application deployment from one technology to another. The *Essential Deployment Metamodel* (EDMM) was hence developed to enable specifying an application deployment in a technology-agnostic manner, in a way that specified deployments can be automatically transformed in the technology-specific deployment artifacts enabling to deploy them with one of the 13 most prominent production-ready deployment technologies. However, not every deployment specified as EDMM model can be executed by all of these deployment technologies, e.g., Kubernetes can actually deploy applications only if their services are containerized. For this reason, this paper introduces the *EDMM Tailoring Support System* (EDMM TSS), which enables determining whether an application deployment can be deployed with a target technology and if this is not the case, recommending and applying model adaptations to enable deploying the application on the desired target technology. We also present a prototype implementation of the EDMM TSS, which is plugged in the existing *EDMM Modeling and Transformation Framework*. Moreover, we present a case study showcasing the overall benefits of the resulting EDMM-based deployment support system.

Keywords: Deployment automation · Deployment modeling · Model transformation · Essential deployment metamodel · EDMM

1 Introduction

The widespread acceptance of cloud computing and DevOps resulted in a plethora of different *deployment automation technologies* [46]. These aim at establishing highly automated deployment processes, since manual deployments of complex multi-service applications are cumbersome and error-prone [24,34]. By describing the services and infrastructure components of an application in reusable deployment models, a repeatable end-to-end automation can be established [2,30].

© Springer Nature Switzerland AG 2022
D. Ferguson et al. (Eds.): CLOSER 2021, CCIS 1607, pp. 1–24, 2022.
https://doi.org/10.1007/978-3-031-21637-4_1

Application deployments are typically modelled declaratively, i.e., by specifying the structure of an application and the desired state into which an application or parts thereof have to be transferred [17, 46]. The declarative approach is indeed supported by the most prominent deployment automation technologies such as AWS CloudFormation, Chef, Juju, Kubernetes, Puppet, and Terraform [46]. However, at the same time, these declarative deployment technologies differ significantly in supported features, deployment mechanisms, and in the supported modeling languages for describing an application deployment [19]. Standards, e.g., the Topology and Orchestration Specification for Cloud Applications (TOSCA) [33], have been proposed to ensure the portability of application deployments from a technology to another. However, most providers and deployment technologies are currently not supporting such standards [38]. This makes it difficult (i) to compare technologies based on their capabilities to select a deployment technology that is suited to accomplish given requirements and (ii) to migrate an application deployment from one technology to another.

To tackle the aforementioned issues, we conducted a systematic review of the 13 most prominent declarative deployment technologies to distill the essential elements common in their modelling languages to define the declarative *Essential Deployment Metamodel (EDMM)* [46], which represents the smallest common denominator of all these technologies. An EDMM model is actually a graph consisting of typed nodes, which represent the components of the application to be deployed, and weighted edges between them representing the typed relationships. Both are also enriched with properties to specify the desired deployment configuration of a component or relationship. We also presented the *EDMM Modeling and Transformation Framework* [43–45], which enables (1) graphically editing EDMM models and (2) automatically transforming technology-agnostic EDMM models into technology-specific deployment models of a desired target technology such as Kubernetes, Terraform, or CloudFormation. Moreover, we have extended the EDMM Framework to support splitting a single EDMM model in order to deploy it using multiple different deployment technologies that are coordinated by the framework [43]. Thus, EDMM models are, in general, portable regarding the actual deployment technology executing them based on such transformations —and even more, multiple technologies can be combined to execute a deployment that is specified by a single EDMM model. Notably, to deploy the same application on different sets of target technologies, the same EDMM model can be processed by simply re-running the EDMM transformation, which enables generating the corresponding technology-specific models.

However, not every deployment specified as EDMM model can be actually executed by all of these deployment technologies: not all existing deployment automation technologies can deploy arbitrary kinds of components on arbitrary kinds of host infrastructures and services. Thus, while the EDMM Transformation Framework in general is capable of transforming EDMM models into technology-specific models, also the *modelled content* needs to be considered: if the target technology cannot deploy what is semantically modelled in the EDMM model, the model transformation cannot be executed and the portability and technology-agnostic character of EDMM gets lost. For example, if the EDMM model specifies the deployment of a Java function on AWS Beanstalk, this part of the EDMM model cannot be executed by Kubernetes as it is not able to deploy applications on Amazon Beanstalk. Thus, the respective part in the EDMM model cannot be transformed into a target model for Kubernetes that is semantically equivalent. While we have already extended the EDMM Framework by a *Decision Support System* [45] that detects such problems and informs the developer that an EDMM model cannot be transformed to, e.g., Kubernetes files, often only small changes to the EDMM model would be sufficient to make the deployment with a certain technology possible. For example, packaging the Java application into a Docker container would enable Kubernetes to run this application. On the other hand, even such small model adaptations require technical expertise, and they are costly and error-prone, given that they are manually performed by a developer.

Therefore, this article presents the *EDMM Tailoring Support System* (EDMM TSS), which enables semi-automatically tailoring an EDMM model to the capabilities of a certain deployment technology if the deployment cannot be executed as modelled by this technology. The *Tailoring Support System* is realized as an extension of the *EDMM Modeling and Transformation Framework* and automatically detects the parts in the EDMM model that cannot be executed by a desired target deployment technology and suggests possible model adaptations. The system allows the user to select the desired adaptation and executes it fully automatically, e.g., our example introduced before could be rewritten by the EDMM TSS in a way that the Java application gets packaged into a Docker container and the Beanstalk node gets exchanged by a Kubernetes node. Thus, by tailoring the original EDMM model and, if necessary, the involved deployment artifacts, the application gets deployable by Kubernetes. As a result, this approach significantly contributes to the portability of EDMM models.

To validate the practical feasibility of the presented approach, we prototypically extended the EDMM Framework by this new feature. Moreover, we assess the overall EDMM-based deployment approach by running a case study based on the open source application *PetClinic* [39]. In the case study, we compare the effort needed to deploy PetClinic with and without the EDMM Framework as well as the effort required to migrate an existing deployment from one deployment technology to another. The effort is measured in terms of the lines of code and files that have to be written, updated, and deleted, as well as in terms of the programming and modelling languages that are to be known. The results of our measurements show that the overall EDMM approach, together with the newly introduced EDMM TSS, reduce application developers' efforts.

Paper Structure. Section 2 provides some background and a motivating example. Sections 3 and 4 illustrate the EDMM approach to technology-agnostic application deployment and its actual implementation, respectively. Section 5 presents a case study-based assessment of the EDMM approach. Sections 6 and 7 conclude the paper by discussing related work and drawing some concluding remarks.

Editorial Note. The Essential Deployment Metamodel (EDMM) was first presented in [46], and a first implementation of the EDMM Modeling and Transformation framework was presented in [44]. The framework was then extended in [45] to support SaaS reuse and PaaS-based deployment, and in [43] to coordinate multiple different technologies to deploy an application.

This paper extends our previous work [43–46] by introducing the *Tailoring Support System* in the EDMM Framework, by presenting for the first time the usability and scope of the integrated EDMM Framework, and by assessing —by means of a case study—

how effectively the EDMM Framework can support researchers and practitioners working with multi-service application deployments. In detail, Sects. 3 and 4 were obtained by merging the corresponding discussions in [43–46] and by extending such discussion to describe the newly introduced *EDMM Tailoring Support*. Section 5 is instead brand new.

2   Background and Motivation

In this section, we provide the background and terms needed to present our work, as well as a simple yet effective example motivating our work.

2.1   Deployment Models, Deployment Technologies, and EDMM

For automating the deployment of an application, *deployment models* are typically used to describe the desired result: in general, there is a distinction between *imperative deployment models* and *declarative deployment models* [17,36]. Declarative models declare exactly *what* is the desired state into which an application or parts thereof must be transferred to. In contrast, imperative models define the exact process of *how* the desired state is reached using executable workflows or programmatic actions. Hence, a declarative deployment model specifies the structure of components to be deployed and specifies the desired state in the form of properties or configurations for those components, but it requires a deployment technology that interprets the model and derives the exact order of operations to reach this state. For example, in Terraform an application developer creates a set of files defining the cloud resources the application to be deployed requires. Terraform, when executing the application deployment, analyzes the resource definitions and derives a workflow having exact steps and actions required to roll-out the desired state.

In industry and research, declarative deployment models are widely accepted as the most appropriate approach for application deployment and configuration management [23]. As a result, a plethora of different technologies have been developed following this approach such as Chef, Puppet, AWS CloudFormation, Terraform, and Kubernetes. However, application systems are often in constant change and, besides the major effort for adapting the application itself, the associated deployment models must be adapted using different or additional deployment technologies [37]. Deployment technologies are heterogeneous regarding supported features and modeling languages [46], and this could result in major efforts whenever an application and its actual deployment have to be adapted to changes in the application requirements. Therefore, it is crucial to postpone as late as possible the choice of which deployment technology to use. An even better approach for application developers is to define their application structure and desired state in a technology-agnostic manner, e.g., by exploiting a normalized metamodel. With a normalized modeling of the application and of its desired state, one could indeed automatically generate the deployment artifacts needed to deploy the application using a given deployment technology.

In our previous work [46], a systematic review of widely used deployment technologies revealed the *Essential Deployment Metamodel* (EDMM). EDMM provides a normalized metamodel as a technology-independent baseline for deployment automation

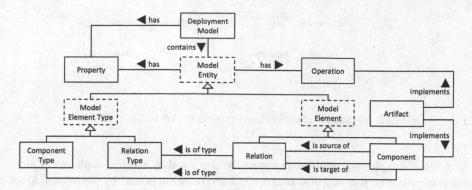

Fig. 1. The Essential Deployment Metamodel (EDMM) [46].

and provides a common understanding of declarative deployment models. EDMM comprises the essential parts supported by production-ready deployment automation technologies and facilitates the transformation in different concrete technologies by a semantic mapping, which avoids deployment technology lock-in. In particular, EDMM defines *Components* as physical, functional, or logical units of an application (cf. Fig. 1). Further, *Relations* are defined as directed physical, functional, or logical dependencies between exactly two components. Both can be typed using *Component Types* and *Relation Types* to express reusable entities that specify a certain semantic. Further, EDMM defines *Properties* as a way to describe the current state or prescribe the desired target state or configuration of a component or relation. Moreover, *Operations* are used in declarative deployment models to define executable procedures performed to manage a component or relation. Such operations provide hook points and are executed by deployment technologies to implement certain requirements during application deployment. Finally, EDMM also defines *Artifacts* such that an artifact implements a component or operation and is therefore required for the execution of the application deployment as well as the final application system.

2.2 Motivating Scenario

As motivating scenario we consider the *PetClinic* application [39]. A possible deployment for the PetClinic application is shown in Fig. 2, where the Pet Clinic service is shown in the center hosted on AWS Beanstalk, the platform as a service (PaaS) offering by Amazon Web Services (AWS). The Pet Clinic service connects to a Database, realized by a fully managed database platform, viz., Amazon Aurora, which is a managed MySQL Database as a Service (DBaaS) offering by AWS. Both Pet Clinic and Database have an artifact attached (cf. Fig. 2), which is, for example, a packaged JAR file in case of the Java application and a SQL file containing the actual database schema and initial data in case of the database component. The left hand side of Fig. 2 depicts a software as a service (SaaS) offering. For this scenario, we envision the usage of a managed authentication service to provide single sign-on between different applications. The Pet Clinic service, therefore, needs to connect or redirect users to this authentication service to authenticate and authorize them.

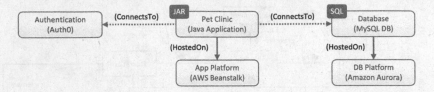

Fig. 2. An example of application deployment modelled with EDMM.

Even if simple, this application cannot be deployed by various deployment technologies. As it is, this scenario is actually only fully supported by Terraform, since Terraform provides different the necessary plugins for managing the different IaaS, PaaS, and SaaS services therein [46]. Other deployment automation technologies may support the specified deployment only partly, e.g., AWS CloudFormation, Ansible, and Chef are capable to deploy the Pet Clinic application on AWS Beanstalk. Some other deployment automation technologies may intead not support the specified deployment in any of its parts, e.g., Kubernetes.

Thus, to fully automate the deployment, we developed a decision support system to determine which declarative deployment technologies can be used to fully deploy a given application deployment model. It is important that application developers receive early deployability feedback immediately while modeling the application. Further, to overcome the technology-specific differences, EDMM as a normalized metamodel provides a solid baseline for deployment automation research and a common understanding of declarative deployment models. The knowledge of essential parts supported by well-known technologies facilitates transformation to different deployment technologies, which avoids deployment technology lock-in.

At the same time, the decision support system we developed does not support adapting an EDMM model to get deployable by a technology that is currently not supporting it. This limits the portability of an existing EDMM model, which can only get deployed on the subset of technologies currently supporting its deployment. Therefore, in this paper, we present an extension of the decision support system: we actually introduce a *Tailoring Support System* that, given an EDMM model and a target deployment automation technologies, enables adapting the EDMM model so that it can get deployed on the target technology. This is done by essentially replacing components that cannot be deployed with topology fragments that are fully supported by a target technology, e.g., replacing Docker containers with web servers hosted on virtual machines when the target technology is IaaS-based and does not support Docker.

3   Extending the EDMM Approach with Tailoring Support

In this section, we introduce our *Tailoring Support* and position it within the overall EDMM approach, whose other parts were separately presented in our previous work [43–45]. The overall EDMM approach enables transforming a technology-independent deployment model based on EDMM into a *deployment technology-specific model* (DTSM) while ensuring supportability by respective deployment technologies. As depicted in Fig. 3, the overall approach is structured in four steps: (1) creating a

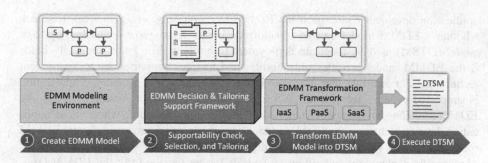

Fig. 3. Production-ready deployment automation by the transformation of EDMM Models into deployment technology-specific models (DTSMs) while ensuring their transformability w.r.t. to features and capabilities of a deployment technology.

technology-independent EDMM model, (2) checking whether a model is supported to be deployed by a deployment technology and, if not, adapting it to achieve compatibility, (3) transforming the EDMM model into a DTSM of a specific deployment technology, and (4) executing the DTSM by coordinating deployment technology native tooling. Step (2), highlighted in darker gray in Fig. 3, is where our newly introduced *Tailoring Support* is used. Such a *Tailoring Support* indeed enables not only checking whether an EDMM model is supported by a target technology, but also adapting it to get supported when this is not the case.

3.1 Step 1: Technology-Independent Application Modeling

The deployment of a multi-service application is specified in EDMM to provide a normalized and technology-independent model. The model is composed graphically by using the *EDMM Modeling Environment* that we proposed in our previous work [44]. The application developer uses the modeling environment to compose a multi-service application structured, e.g., as depicted in Fig. 2. The creation of certain EDMM components is based on existing types that are provided by the modeling environment. At any time, the resulting model is compliant to the EDMM in YAML specification [42] and can be exported. To improve the modeling experience and to tackle the issue that an application developer needs live feedback whether a certain deployment technology is capable of deploying the current model. Therefore, the modeling environment uses the *EDMM Decision Support Framework* as described in the next section. Essentially, the decision support checks whether a model is supported to be deployed by a given deployment technology. When this is not the case, the *EDMM Tailoring Support System* enables automatically adapting the EDMM model to obtain compatibility with such technology. Notice that the *Tailoring Support System* is newly introduced in this paper, whereas the *Decision Support Framework* (as per our previous work [45]) only enabled detecting whether an EDMM model can be deployed by a certain technology.

3.2 Step 2: Technology Decision Support and Tailoring for EDMM Models

This work newly introduces the *EDMM Tailoring Support System* (TSS) within the *EDMM Decision Support Framework* module shown in Fig. 3. Having the TSS, an application developer can exploit the *EDMM Decision Support Framework* to check whether a EDMM model can be transformed into a *deployment technology-specific model* (DTSM) used by a certain deployment technology. The latter obviously holds if the EDMM model includes only entities and features supported by a deployment technology. For example, the user gets immediate feedback if a modeled application is supported by, e.g., Terraform, AWS CloudFormation, Juju, or Ansible. Hereby, the *EDMM Modeling* environment triggers the decision support module whenever an application developer changes the EDMM model. This module consumes the current EDMM model and checks whether and to which degree the model is transformable into a DTSM of a specific deployment technology. As per its former version [45], the *EDMM Decision Support* only generated a report that was presented to the application developer. Based on this report, the EDMM Framework enabled checking transformability into a specific deployment technology. There was however no support in adapting the EDMM model to get supported by a given technology, if this was not the case [45].

The TSS included in *EDMM Decision Support Framework* comes precisely to that purpose, as it now enables adapting the deployment model when it cannot be transformed in a DTSM for a target deployment automation technology. The report shown to the application developer now also includes recommendations on how to adapt the EDMM model to get fully deployable by a certain target technology. The developer can browse among the possible adaptations and choose the one to apply: once selected, the EDMM model gets automatically updated to incorporate the adaptation. Notice that the enacted adaptation occurs at deployment modelling level, resulting in the possibility to generate a DTSM that can actually be processed by a target technology. Additional refactorings may be needed, e.g., incorporating the binaries and configuration needed to run the components that were included to adapt an unsupported component, if they cannot be automatically generated with the *EDMM Transformation Framework* [44].

3.3 Step 3: Transform EDMM Model into DTSM

For transformation, the EDMM model is consumed by the *EDMM Transformation Framework*, which we presented in [44], and which can transform EDMM models into the deployable artifacts that allow deploying the specified application on the selected deployment automation technology. For example, we developed transformation rules for transforming IaaS components to AWS EC2 instances, PaaS components to AWS CloudFormation components, or SaaS components into their Terraform's counterpart. More generally, for each of the 13 most prominent deployment automation technologies, the *EDMM Transformation Framework* [44] includes plugins that are able to transform the specified EDMM components into their technology-specific counterparts, if a given technology is supporting them, of course.

3.4 Step 4: Technology-specific Deployment Execution

The *EDMM Transformation Framework* outputs a so-called *deployment technology-specific model* (DTSM). For example, in Terraform this will be a configuration that consists of a set of *.tf files referencing respective artifacts to deploy. If an application is to be deployed by only one target technology, there will be only one DTSM, which can be directly provided to the target technology to enact the specified deployment.

The EDMM Framework also support partitioning the deployment of an application among multiple target deployment automation technologies, thanks to the extension we presented in our previous work [43]. This is done by exploiting the *EDMM Transformation Framework* [44] to transform each different portion of the EDMM model to a DTSM enabling to deploy it with the corresponding target technology. As we shown in [43], the EDMM Framework also derives an appropriate deployment order for the application portions, one that enables deploying an application service only when all the services it depends on have already been deployed. Such deployment order is then enforced by the EDMM Framework, essentially by instructing the target deployment technologies so as that services in the obtained DTSMs are deployed according to the derived deployment order.

4   The Extended *EDMM Modeling and Transformation Framework*

In this section, we present the architecture of the integrated EDMM Framework and its current prototypical implementation. More precisely, we recap the existing architecture and prototype implementation of the EDMM Framework, whilst also illustrating how the *EDMM Tailoring Support*, newly introduced in this paper, plugs into the architecture and was added to the prototype implementation.

4.1   Architecture of the Extended EDMM Framework

Figure 4 shows the overall system architecture of the proposed extension of the EDMM framework, comprising the various components needed to realize the EDMM-based deployment approach described in Sect. 3. Light gray components represent new components while the shaded component represents the existing plugins that have been extended in the course of this work.

The *Modeling Tool* is a web-based modeling environment exploiting a *REST API* to retrieve and update the EDMM framework data, which is stored in the *Types Repository*. This repository contains the deployment models created by users, as well as the reusable EDMM component types that an application developer can use for modeling and provide the respective technical and platform abstractions. An application developer uses these types in the *Modeling Tool* to graphically compose the structure of the EDMM model, which is then stored and manged in the *Models Repository*.

To check the transformation support and facilitate decision support, the *Decision Support* component, first presented in [45], was extended with the *Tailoring Support* as depicted in Fig. 4, whilst the actual transformation of EDMM models into DTSMs is delegated to the *Transformation* component [44]. Both components employ a plugin architecture that supports the integration of various deployment technologies in an extensible and pluggable way. Each plugin employs the knowledge whether a certain component in the EDMM model is supported by the respective target technology or not. The *Decision Support* component is able to utilize the plugins to check a given EDMM model and to produce a report what components (and component types) are not

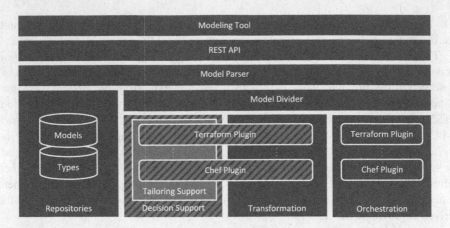

Fig. 4. Integrated architecture of the EDMM Framework. The newly introduced component is highlighted in grey, whilst extended components are shaded.

supported. Further, the plugins carry the logic and transformation rules exploited by the *Tailoring Support* to adapt the model to work with a given technology, and by the *Transformation Framework* to transform an EDMM model into a deployment technology-specific model (DTSM). The latter includes the creation of respective technology-specific directory structures, files, and artifacts. The *Model Parser* consumes a textual EDMM model in YAML and creates an internal data structure used by the *Decision Support* and *Transformation* components, and by the respective plugins.

The support for deploying a multi-service application with multiple deployment automation technologies, which we presented in our previous work [43], is realized by the *Model Divider* component, which essentially enables partitioning a single application in the portions to be deployed with different technologies. Different portions are then analyzed differently by the *Decision Support*, which also provides different recommendations for adapting the portions to get deployed on target technologies, if needed, by relying on the newly introduced *Tailoring Support*. This is realized by essentially partitioning the internal representation created by the *Model Parser* into different portions to be deployed differently. The different portions of the original model are then checked, adapted, and transformed separately, respectively by the *Decision Support*, *Tailoring Support*, and *Transformation Framework*.

Finally, the transformation of models into DTSMs and the actual deployment are realized by the components *Transformation* [44] and *Orchestration* [43], respectively. As anticipated above, the *Transformation* component uses a plugin architecture to supports the integration of various deployment technologies in an extensible way. Each plugin carry the logic and transformation rules to transform an EDMM model into a DTSM, which includes the creation of respective technology-specific directory structures, files, and artifacts based on the respective DSL.

The *Orchestration* component is also realized as a plugin architecture, with each plugin wrapping the logic to interact with a given deployment technology, e.g., by exploiting the technology's SDK or CLI. The *Orchestration* component determines the deployment order as described in Sect. 3, and it then invokes the orchestration plugins to enforce such deployment order. Once invoked, a plugin essentially realizes a sub-process that executes the DTSM using the given input data and retrieves runtime information, e.g., IP addresses, after the successful execution. Whenever the execution of a plugin completes, the *Orchestration* component populates and stores runtime information based on what returned by a plugin. It also determines the input information, i.e., property values and runtime information, required by plugins to successfully get executed. The *Orchestration* component is hence aware of the overall EDMM model, the EDMM model fragments, the deployment groups, and the runtime information propagated back to the system after each deployment task, i.e., after each invocation to an orchestration plugin.

4.2 Prototypical Implementation

In this section, we illustrate a prototypical implementation of the proposed approach and the extended system architecture. We base our prototype on two existing components: (i) Eclipse Winery [28] to realize the *EDMM Modeling Environment* and (ii) the EDMM Transformation Framework [44] to realize the *Transformation* component of the EDMM Framework. Such components were extended in [45] by introducing the *Decision Support*, and in [43] to incorporate what needed to enable partitioning an EDMM model across multiple technologies. In this paper, we further extend the prototypical implementation of EDMM framework by including a prototype of the newly proposed *EDMM Tailoring Support System*.

Extended Prototypical Implementation. Eclipse Winery is a web-based environment to graphically model TOSCA-based application topologies. It provides a *back-end* to manage component and relation types, their property definitions, operations, and artifacts. Further, it provides a *Topology Modeler* enabling the graphical composition of application deployment models including the specification of the components' properties. Even though Winery was initially developed as TOSCA modeling environment, in previous work we showed that EDMM can be mapped to TOSCA [47,48].

In this paper, we extended Winery's Topology Modeler to not only provide a live checking of application models, but also to enable tailoring EDMM models for them to get supported by a given target deployment technology, if this was not the case. As for its latest version befor this paper, Winery already called the *Decision Support* component whenever the application developer changes the EDMM model, e.g., when adding or removing components. The latter returns information on which deployment automation technologies are supporting the deployment of the components in the specified EDMM model. Winery uses such information to highlight the technologies that are not supporting a specified deployment, and the components due to which this happens.

To enable adapting the components causing a target technology to not support the deployment of an EDMM model, we developed a rule-based system. Intuitively speaking, each rule prescribes how to transform each unsupported component type (among those available in the *Types Repository*—cf. Fig. 4) to a composition of component types providing the same functionality, whilst however being supported by the target technology. Such a rule-based system was realised by still exploiting the plugin architecture of the EDMM Framework, by essentially extending each of the available plugins with a set of rules for transforming unsupported types to supported type compositions.

To use the prototype,[1] we also created a Docker Compose configuration able to start a pre-configured and ready-to-use EDMM Modeling, Decision Support, and Transformation System. All changes and improvements in the course of this paper have been merged to the *master* branches of the respective repositories.

Using the Prototype. In this section, we show the overall modeling, decision support, and transformation flow of our implemented prototype. The flow is explained based on a modeling example that follows our motivating scenario in Fig. 2. For simplifying presentation, we chose Terraform as the only target deployment technology.

After running the Docker-based deployment of the EDMM Framework extended with tailoring support, application developers can access the *EDMM Modeling Tool* to model their desired application structure. As depicted in Fig. 5, the user composes the structure by drag-and-drop desired components to the canvas. Additionally, users define respective relations between them by connecting the components. To facilitate decision support, we implemented live modeling feedback directly in the modeling environment (cf. 1 in Fig. 5). Whenever, the overall model is changed, the *Decision Support* component is triggered. All available plugins of the *Decision Support* are queried to check whether the current model contains unsupported components. The modeling environments retrieves the result and presents it to the application developer. Application developers can also exploit the feedback from the *Decision Support* component to adapt their deployment to match a desired technology which is not the in the scenario depicted in Fig. 5, as the modelled deployment can actually be transformed into Terraform. The same would not hold if targeting Chef, for which the "adapt" option is available in our scenario (cf. Fig. 5). In that case, developers can exploit the *Tailoring Support* to adapt the modelled deployment and get it supported by Chef..

After modelling the desired deployment, developers can export the resulting EDMM model in YAML, according to the EDMM YAML specification [42]. Application developers can also enact the transformation by selecting the desired and supported deployment technology (cf. 2 in Fig. 5). The output of the system is then transformed according to the need a corresponding deployment technology requires. For example, in case of Terraform, it will be a ready to use working directory containing Terraform configuration files (cf. 3 in Fig. 5). In Fig. 6, we show an excerpt a modeled EDMM-based SaaS component and its mapping to the actual Terraform resource.

Lastly, the application developer is able to execute the actual deployment using the tools and interfaces provided by the deployment technology. For instance, Terraform provides a CLI to "apply" the generated configuration. At this point, application developers can use their well-known development environments and tools to deploy and manage their applications (cf. 4 in Fig. 5). For example, the generated deployment artifacts can be versioned in revision control systems, such as Git, to facilitate the use of automated CI/CD pipelines.

---

[1] https://github.com/UST-EDMM.

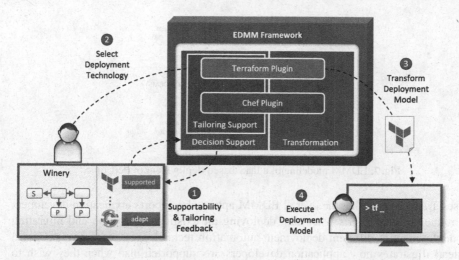

Fig. 5. Prototype flow demonstrating the modeling, decision and tailoring support, and transformation of an EDMM model to Terraform.

EDMM in YAML	Transformation to Terraform
| ```
components:
  # other components
  # omitted for brevity
  authentication:
    type: auth0
    properties:
      domain: example.test
      identifier: ...
      scopes: user,admin
      client_id: abc
      client_secret: xyz123abc
``` | ```
resource "auth0_resource_server" "authentication" {
  name         = "authentication"
  identifier   = "..."
  signing_alg  = "RS256"
  scopes {
    value = "user"
  }
  scopes {
    value = "admin"
  }
  ...
}
``` |

Fig. 6. Terraform transformation mapping [45].

5 Case Study and Evaluation

We hereafter present and discuss different deployments of the PetClinic application (cf. Sect. 2), with the aim of demonstrating how the EDMM approach, realized through the *EDMM Modelling and Transformation Framework* eases deploying multi-service applications. In particular, we consider four different deployments of PetClinic, which correspond to four subsequent deployments of this application, i.e., starting from its first deployment and going through its migration to different deployment automation technologies. The four considered deployments are indeed the following:

1. Deploying PetClinic with Kubernetes (Sect. 5.1).
2. Migrating the deployment of PetClinic from Kubernetes to Ansible, CloudFormation, or Terraform (Sect. 5.2).
3. Adapting the Terraform deployment of PetClinic to run on PaaS platforms (Sect. 5.3).
4. Adapting and migrating the deployment of PetClinic from Terraform to Puppet (Sect. 5.4)

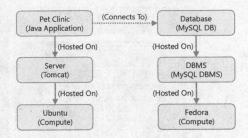

Fig. 7. EDMM modeling of a IaaS-based deployment of PetClinic.

Cases 1 and 2 show that the overall EDMM approach supports application developers by reducing their efforts when first deploying an existing application and migrating its deployment to different deployment automation technologies, respectively. Case 3 instead illustrates how application developers are supported also when they wish to change the specified deployment of an application, namely in the case when they wish to deploy the application components on different types of cloud offerings. Finally, case 4 evaluates the support provided by the newly introduced *Tailoring Support*, by showing how it can be used to automatically adapt an existing deployment to work with a deployment automation technology that was not supporting it.[2]

To actually measure the support provided by the EDMM approach, in all cases we compare the manual writing of the technology-specific files needed to deploy PetClinic with the use of the EDMM Framework to specify the same deployment and generate the needed artifacts. The metrics used to evaluate the effort in all considered deployments are the following: number of *lines of code*, number of *files*, and programming *languages* used. As for the lines of codes and files, we shall distinguish those that have been *added* (a), *changed* (c), and *deleted* (d). While such metrics can be directly computed on the manually written technology-specific files, we measure them against the output EDMM files generated by the EDMM modeling environment, as if they were to be manually written. The rationale behind this decision is that comparing UI interactions with lines of code would have instead been unfair.

5.1   First Deployment of PetClinic

This first case was intended to show that the EDMM approach supports application developers by reducing their efforts when first deploying an existing application. We hence considered the open source PetClinic application, which we wished to deploy according to the deployment specification shown in Fig. 7: the Pet Clinic web application was to be installed in a Tomcat Server and connected to the MySQL Database. The latter was managed by a MySQL DBMS. Finally, the Server and the DBMS were installed on two different compute nodes.

We manually specified such deployment in Kubernetes by manually developing the two Dockerfiles for running the two software stacks forming the considered deployment, as well as the Kubernetes manifest files needed to enact such deployment. We also

---

[2] The EDMM and technology-specific sources for all the considered deployment cases are publicly available on GitHub at https://github.com/di-unipi-socc/edmm-case-studies.

Table 1. Lines of code, files, and languages used for deploying PetClinic with Kubernetes. *a*, *c*, and *d* are used to denote the lines of code/files added, changed, and deleted, respectively.

	Lines of Code				**Files**				
	a	*c*	*d*	*total*	*a*	*c*	*d*	*total*	**Languages**
without EDMM	152	0	0	152	7	0	0	7	Kubernetes, Dockerfile
with EDMM	131	0	0	131	1	0	0	1	EDMM

modeled the deployment with the EDMM Framework, and we exploited its transformation capabilities to automatically generate the files needed for enacting the deployment in Kubernetes. After checking that both deployments were effectively working, we measured the lines of code, files, and programming languages employed to specify and enact the Kubernetes deployment of PetClinic with and without our EDMM-based approach. The results are reported in Table 1.

By looking at Table 1, one may conclude that exploiting EDMM is already more convenient if compared to manually writing the Dockerfiles and Kubernetes manifest files needed to enact the desired deployment of PetClinic. At the same time, we must say that this come at the price of suitably configuring the EDMM modeling environment to support modeling the desired application deployment. The EDMM modeling environment indeed requires service types to be defined for enabling them to get included in the specification of an application deployment. While Compute, Tomcat, MysqlDbms and MysqlDatabase are available by default, the PetClinicApp was to be defined using the UI by extending the existing WebApplication type. The artifacts and binaries implementing the PetClinic application were to be added too, to enable linking them while modeling the EDMM specification of the desired application deployment.

In addition, the application developers are required to learn the EDMM modeling language, whose online available support is much less than that available for Kubernetes and Docker. The latter are indeed well-known production ready technologies for which plenty of documentation is available online, together with blogs, forums, and tutorials explaining how to use them. This is just to clarify that, even if Table 1 suggests that using EDMM for the first deployment of an application may already be more convenient, this may unfortunately not be the case. The same does not hold when migrating the deployment of an application to a different technology: EDMM indeed results to be much more convenient in the case of technology migrations after the first deployment, as we will showcase in the following sections.

5.2 Migrating the Deployment of PetClinic to Other Technologies

The second case was intended to show that the EDMM approach supports application developers by reducing their efforts when migrating the deployment of an existing application to different deployment automation technologies. We hence report on the effort needed to migrate the deployment of PetClinic (i) from Kubernetes to Ansible, (ii) from Ansible to CloudFormation, and (iii) from CloudFormation to Terraform. In all the three cases, we manually written the files needed to enact the deployment on the target technology by starting from the files already written for deploying PetClinic with the previously used technology. Unfortunately, we always had to rewrite the deployment files from scratch, other than in case (iii), where we were able to adapt one shell script

Table 2. Lines of code, files, and languages used for migrating the deployment of PetClinic from Kubernetes to Ansible. *a*, *c*, and *d* are used to denote the lines of code/files added, changed, and deleted, respectively.

	Lines of Code				Files				Languages
	a	*c*	*d*	*total*	*a*	*c*	*d*	*total*	
without EDMM	89	0	152	241	1	0	7	8	Ansible DSL
with EDMM	0	0	0	0	0	0	0	0	—

Table 3. Lines of code, files, and languages used for migrating the deployment of PetClinic from Ansible to CloudFormation. *a*, *c*, and *d* are used to denote the lines of code/files added, changed, and deleted, respectively.

	Lines of Code				Files				Languages
	a	*c*	*d*	*total*	*a*	*c*	*d*	*total*	
without EDMM	333	0	89	422	3	0	1	4	CloudFormation DSL, bash
with EDMM	0	0	0	0	0	0	0	0	—

written to deploy PetClinic with CloudFormation and reuse it in the target Terraform deployment. When using EDMM, instead, we were not required to touch the EDMM specification, but rather to just "press the button" for generating the needed deployment artifacts starting from the same specification. Table 2, Table 3, Table 4 show this: Table 2 report the lines of code, files, and programming languages involved in migrating the deployment from Kubernetes to Ansible, Table 3 reports those measured for the migration from Ansible to CloudFormation, and Table 4 reports those measured for the migration from CloudFormation to Terraform.

The numbers in Table 2, Table 3, and Table 4 highlight the lack of portability of deployment artifacts, which are inherently technology-specific, as each deployment automation technology has its own specific language and way of describing the state of the model. In addition, the expertise required for enacting the migration differs in all the three cases. Indeed, when we "manually" changed deployment automation technology, we were required to map the deployment modeling of one technology to that of the target technology. The language metric helps noting this, as we first had to translate the Kubernetes manifest files to files written in the Ansible DSL, which were then translated to files written with the CloudFormation DSL, which were finally translated to the Terraform DSL. Again, each time we migrated the deployment to a different technology, we had to rewrite all deployment files almost from scratch and we were required to learn and understand a different DSL at each migration. With the EDMM-based approach, instead, we were able to reuse the same file we developed initially (cf. Sect. 5.1), which means that we were required to know only the EDMM modeling language and to specify the deployment only once.

5.3   Migrating to a PaaS Deployment of PetClinic

The third case intended to illustrate that application developers are supported also when they wish to change the specified deployment of an application. We hence considered

Table 4. Lines of code, files, and languages used for migrating the deployment of PetClinic from CloudFormation to Terraform. a, c, and d are used to denote the lines of code/files added, changed, and deleted, respectively.

	Lines of Code				Files				
	a	c	d	total	a	c	d	total	Languages
without EDMM	181	7	333	514	1	1	2	4	Terraform DSL, bash
with EDMM	0	0	0	0	0	0	0	0	—

Table 5. Lines of code, files, and languages used for migrating the Terraform deployment of PetClinic from IaaS-based to PaaS-based. a, c, and d are used to denote the lines of code/files added, changed, and deleted, respectively.

	Lines of Code				Files				
	a	c	d	total	a	c	d	total	Languages
without EDMM	65	0	173	238	1	1	1	3	Terraform DSL, bash
with EDMM	59	0	78	137	0	1	0	1	EDMM

the case of migrating the deployment of PetClinic from the IaaS-based deployment in Fig. 7 to the PaaS-based deployment in Fig. 8, while at the same time fixing the deployment automation technology to the last used, i.e., Terraform. In the case of manually adapting the Terraform deployment, we manually updated the files specifying such deployment in such a way that the web application and the database were to be hosted on instances of AWS Beanstalk and AWS Aurora, respectively. In the case of doing this with EDMM, we exploited the support given by the EDMM Framework's modeling environment to replace services and obtain the topology shown in Fig. 8. After checking that both deployments were working, we measured the lines of code, files, and programming languages employed to specify and enact the PaaS-based Terraform deployment of PetClinic with and without our EDMM-based approach (cf. Table 5).

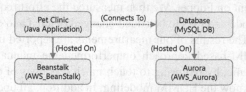

Fig. 8. EDMM modeling of a PaaS-based deployment of PetClinic.

By looking at Table 5, one can readily observe that exploiting the support given by our EDMM-based approach was sensibly reducing the effort required to enact the desired migration. This is even more evident if we consider that all reasoning and updates performed were done with the graphical support given by the EDMM Framework's modeling environment and with the support given by the decision support component integrated with such environment. The same does not hold when performing the

Table 6. Lines of code, files, and languages used for migrating the deployment of PetClinic from Terraform to Puppet. *a*, *c*, and *d* are used to denote the lines of code/files added, changed, and deleted, respectively.

| | Lines of Code | | | | Files | | | | |
	a	*c*	*d*	*total*	*a*	*c*	*d*	*total*	**Languages**
without EDMM	168	0	80	248	11	1	1	13	Puppet DSL
with EDMM	78	0	59	137	0	1	0	1	EDMM

same updates manually, where the reasoning is to be done "on paper" or by exploiting tools that are not natively integrated with Terraform.

5.4 Migrating to a Technology Not Supporting the Deployment

The fourth and final case intended to evaluate the support given by the newly included *Tailoring Support* when adapting an application deployment to enable deploying it with a technology that is not supporting such deployment. We hence started from the EDMM modeling of the PaaS-based deployment of PetClinic and we considered the case of deploying the application with Puppet. The decision support component alerted us, showing that the deployment automation technology we were targeting was not supporting the deployment modeling because of the AWS Beanstalk and AWS Aurora services. The decision support component also informed us that we could have replaced such services with software stacks, i.e., a web server on top of a compute instance in the case of AWS Beanstalk, and a DBMS on top of a compute instance in the case of AWS Aurora. We hence instructed the EDMM Framework's modeling environment to automatically apply such replacements, which resulted in a deployment modeling similar to that in Fig. 7. We were then able to automatically generate the artifacts to enact the desired deployment on Puppet.

We did the same migration manually, i.e., we started from the Terraform deployment of PetClinic obtained in Sect. 5.3 and we manually generated the files needed to enact the desired deployment on Puppet. We then measured the effort required in both cases, in terms of lines of code and files to be added/changed/deleted and of the programming languages involved. The results of our measurements are reported in Table 6.

Again, our EDMM-based approach outperformed the manual adaptation of the deployment of PetClinic, by requiring to touch much less lines of codes and files, and by only requiring to know the EDMM modeling. In addition, all updates were automatically suggested by the *Tailoring Support* component in the EDMM Framework's modeling environment. The same would not have held if we were doing the same migration only manually. In such a case, we would have been required to understand that Puppet cannot deploy on PaaS platforms such as AWS Beanstalk and AWS Aurora, as well as to figure out how to replace such services to enable deploying PetClinic with Puppet. Both things would have resulted in time-consuming and error-prone processes, which were saved by the fact that the *Tailoring Support* component was automatically recommending us on how to proceed.

6 Related Work

How to automatically deploy multi-service applications on cloud platforms is a well-know problem [10,27,41]. Most of the existing approaches for enabling cloud deployment automation follow a declarative approach [4], with the OASIS standard TOSCA [32,33] being one of the most prominent examples in this direction. TOSCA provides a standardized language for specifying multi-service applications in a portable way. Specified applications can then be deployed on cloud infrastructures, provided that such infrastructures feature runtimes capable of declaratively processing TOSCA application specifications, e.g., OpenTOSCA [5,7]. Our EDMM-based approach differs from TOSCA, as we aim at automatically generating the deployment artifacts needed to deploy an application with an existing technology as it is.

Similar considerations apply to other approaches allowing to declaratively specify the deployment of multi-service applications, e.g., CAMEL [1], Cloud4SOA [25], CoMe4ACloud [9], MODAClouds [15], Panarello et al [35], SeaClouds [8], and trans-cloud [11,12]. They all start from vendor-agnostic application specifications and enable their deployment on heterogeneous clouds. They however also rely on additional components to be featured by targeted clouds, or on ad-hoc middlewares processing application specifications to enact and coordinate the deployment of application services. Our EDMM-based approach also starts from a vendor-agnostic representation of multi-service applications, but it rather automatically generates different artifacts for deploying the same application with different, production-ready deployment automation technologies, in order to directly use such technologies to deploy multi-service applications on heterogeneous clouds.

In this perspective, deployment automation solutions that can be considered closer to ours are those by Di Cosmo et al [13,14] and Guillén et al [20]. They both share our baseline idea of enabling to automate the deployment of a multi-service application by generating concrete deployment artifacts by starting from a vendor-agnostic representation of such application. In particular, Di Cosmo et al [13,14] propose an approach for automatically synthesizing the artifacts needed for deploying a multi-service applications in OpenStack clouds based on a high-level specification of the application and of its desired configuration. Their approach however differs from ours, as they target OpenStack cloud deployments. We instead target 13 different production-ready deployment technologies, each allowing to deploy applications on multiple heterogeneous cloud infrastructures [44], and for which we provide a support for tailoring a specified deployment to work with any of such technologies.

Guillén et al [20] instead propose a framework for developing multi-service applications by decoupling them from the architecture, services, and libraries actually provided by cloud vendors. Based on additional metadata indicating the requirements for an application, the framework by Guillén et al automatically generates cloud compliant software artifacts that can be deployed in the target cloud infrastructures. This approach can hence be considered even closer to ours, as the same vendor-agnostic application can be deployed differently by re-running the framework and instructing it to target different cloud infrastructures. The approach by Guillén et al however differs from ours since it enables deploying applications whose source code is available to the framework, while our EDMM-based approach only requires the application specification and the final packaged software artifacts, whose deployment can be tailored to work with different deployment automation technologies. Our EDMM-based approach can hence be applied to a wider set of scenaria, as we enable application developers to reuse *blackbox* third-party software artifacts or SaaS services to implement the services in their applications. Similar considerations also apply to the deployment automation approach by Alipour and Liu [3], who exploit model-to-model transformation to automatically synthesize cloud-specific deployments for vendor-agnostic applications.

Harzenetter et al [21,22] instead present an approach to model deployments using abstract design patterns, rather than concrete technical components. Harzenetter et al also show that their pattern-based models can be automatically transformed into executable deployment models that contain only technical components and dependencies. Thus, this approach also tackles the portability of deployment models and transforms them. However, in the approach by Harzenetter et al, components and dependencies expressed as patterns are only refined to concrete technologies, not changed as it is required if, e.g., an AWS Beanstalk-based deployment must be executed using Kubernetes. Moreover, the portability aspect in the approach by Harzenetter et al results from high-level, abstract, pattern-based modelling, while in our approach concretely specified deployment models are adapted for a certain target deployment technology.

Similar considerations apply to Breitenbücher et al [6] who presented a pattern-based approach for automatically transforming declarative instance models of running applications into prescriptive desired state models, which can be then executed automatically to bring a running application into the desired state. In their work, management patterns were enriched with transformation logic to transform the content of an instance model to a desired state model. The rationale for these transformations was the need to execute management logic, not to make a deployment model executable using a certain deployment technology as described in this paper. Therefore, the transformation approach proposed by Breitenbücher et al did not take the deployment technology into account and was, therefore, also not able to adapt a deployment for the needs and capabilities of a certain deployment technology

Other deployment automation solutions worth mentioning are the Open Application Model [29] (OAM), Kompose [40] and Compose Object [16]. OAM was recently proposed to enable developers and operators to separately describe containerized applications with a vendor-agnostic representation. OAM allows to describe what containerized services do and how they should be configured. Application specifications can then be completed by configuring the actual runtime environments. Completed OAM application specifications can then be run on Kubernetes with KubeVela [31]. Kompose [40] and Compose Object [16] also enable deploying containerized, multi-service applications on Kubernetes. Kompose [40] does so by automatically generating a Kubernetes deployment for containerized applications specified in Docker Compose, while Compose Object [16] is a Kubernetes plugin for directly running such a kind of applications on Kubernetes clusters. Our EDMM-based approach can not only be used for running containerized multi-service applications on Kubernetes, as we rather support deploying other types of applications on other deployment technologies. In addition, in the case of an application not being deployable with a given technology, we support tailoring the application deployment so that it gets supported by such technology.

Thus, to the best of our knowledge, our EDMM-based approach constitutes the first approach for automatically generating the artifacts to concretely deploy multi-service applications with different existing deployment automation technologies, which also enables reusing *black-box* third-party software and SaaS services to implement some of the application services. It does so by starting from the widely accepted idea of specifying an application in a technology-agnostic way, without requiring cloud providers to support additional runtimes, and by piggybacking on existing, production-ready deployment technology to actually enact application deployments. In addition, our EDMM-based approach is the first also featuring a decision support for adapting applications to enable deploying with technologies that would instead not support their deployment.

In the latter perspective, it is finally worth relating our decision support with other solutions offering decision support for cloud-based application deployments. Farshidi et al [18] provide a DSS to ease selecting the IaaS cloud most suited for deploying an application, based on a multi-criteria decision making problem defined over non-functional requirements, including cost and security. Khajeh-Hosseini et al [26] introduce the Cloud Adoption Toolkit, which enables modelling multi-service application deployments, therein include the application structure, data, infrastructure requirements, and resource usage patterns. The toolkit then reports on cost estimates, benefits, and risks resulting from using different IaaS clouds for enacting the modelled application deployment. Both solution hence support application developers in selecting the IaaS clouds for enacting the deployment of their multi-service application, by taking into account their infrastructure requirements and costs. The objective of the decision support included in the EDMM Framework is different, as it enables adapting multi-service applications to allow deploying them with different declarative deployment automation technologies, which can then be used to deploy the same application on IaaS or PaaS clouds. To the best of our knowledge, such a kind of decision support is first presented here, as the currently existing systems providing decision support for cloud-based application deployments consider application deployments as they are and pick different cloud offerings based on their requirements. We instead enable adapting an application deployment to work with a target technology.

7   Conclusions

We have presented an extension of the EDMM Framework, incorporating a brand new *Tailoring System* to enable tailoring EDMM models to get supported by a target deployment automation technology. We have described the four main functionalities provided by the resulting EDMM Framework, namely (i) a graphical modelling environment enabling users to specify the EDMM model of their application, (ii) supporting developers in adapting EDMM models to get supported by a given technology, (iii) automatically transforming specified EDMM models into DTSMs needed to deploy applications with the desired target deployment technologies, and (iv) coordinating such deployment technologies to concretely enact the desired deployment. We have also presented an assessment of our overall approach on a third-party case study.

The EDMM Framework currently supports the 13 most popular deployment automation technologies [46]. Future work includes extending the list of supported technologies, which can be achieved by developing ad-hoc plugins for each newly introduced technology, given the plugin architecture of the EDMM Framework.

References

1. Achilleos, A.P., et al.: The cloud application modelling and execution language. J. Cloud Comput. **8**(1), 1–25 (2019). https://doi.org/10.1186/s13677-019-0138-7
2. Agrawal, P., Rawat, N.: DevOps: a new approach to cloud development & testing. In: 2019 International Conference on Issues and Challenges in Intelligent Computing Techniques (ICICT), vol. 1, pp. 1–4 (2019). https://doi.org/10.1109/ICICT46931.2019.8977662
3. Alipour, H., Liu, Y.: Model driven deployment of auto-scaling services on multiple clouds. In: 2018 IEEE International Conference on Software Architecture Companion, pp. 93–96. 2018 IEEE International Conference on Software Architecture Companion (ICSA-C 2018) (2018). https://doi.org/10.1109/ICSA-C.2018.00033
4. Bergmayr, A., et al.: A systematic review of cloud modeling languages. ACM Comput. Surv. **51**(1) (2018). https://doi.org/10.1145/3150227
5. Binz, T., et al.: OpenTOSCA – a runtime for TOSCA-based cloud applications. In: Basu, S., Pautasso, C., Zhang, L., Fu, X. (eds.) ICSOC 2013. LNCS, vol. 8274, pp. 692–695. Springer, Heidelberg (2013). https://doi.org/10.1007/978-3-642-45005-1_62
6. Breitenbücher, U., Binz, T., Kopp, O., Leymann, F.: Pattern-based runtime management of composite cloud applications. In: Proceedings of the 3rd International Conference on Cloud Computing and Services Science (CLOSER 2013), pp. 475–482. SciTePress (2013)
7. Breitenbücher, U., et al.: The OpenTOSCA ecosystem - concepts & tools. In: European Space project on Smart Systems, Big Data, Future Internet - Towards Serving the Grand Societal Challenges - Volume 1: EPS Rome 2016, pp. 112–130 (2016). https://doi.org/10.5220/0007903201120130
8. Brogi, A., et al.: EU project seaclouds - adaptive management of service-based applications across multiple clouds. In: Proceedings of the 4th International Conference on Cloud Computing and Services Science, pp. 758–763. SciTePress (2014). https://doi.org/10.5220/0004979507580763
9. Bruneliere., H., Al-Shara., Z., Alvares., F., Lejeune., J., Ledoux., T.: A model-based architecture for autonomic and heterogeneous cloud systems. In: Proceedings of the 8th International Conference on Cloud Computing and Services Science - CLOSER, pp. 201–212. SciTePress (2018). https://doi.org/10.5220/0006773002010212
10. Calheiros, R.N., Ranjan, R., Beloglazov, A., De Rose, C.A.F., Buyya, R.: Cloudsim: a toolkit for modeling and simulation of cloud computing environments and evaluation of resource provisioning algorithms. Softw.: Pract. Exp. **41**(1), 23–50 (2011). https://doi.org/10.1002/spe.995
11. Carrasco, J., Durán, F., Pimentel, E.: Trans-cloud: CAMP/TOSCA-based bidimensional cross-cloud. Comput. Stand. Interfaces **58**, 167–179 (2018). https://doi.org/10.1016/j.csi.2018.01.005
12. Carrasco, J., Durán, F., Pimentel, E.: Live migration of trans-cloud applications. Comput. Stand. Interfaces **69**, 103392 (2020). https://doi.org/10.1016/j.csi.2019.103392
13. Di Cosmo, R., Eiche, A., Mauro, J., Zacchiroli, S., Zavattaro, G., Zwolakowski, J.: Automatic deployment of services in the cloud with Aeolus blender. In: Barros, A., Grigori, D., Narendra, N.C., Dam, H.K. (eds.) ICSOC 2015. LNCS, vol. 9435, pp. 397–411. Springer, Heidelberg (2015). https://doi.org/10.1007/978-3-662-48616-0_28
14. Di Cosmo, R., et al.: Automated synthesis and deployment of cloud applications. In: Proceedings of the 29th ACM/IEEE International Conference on Automated Software Engineering, pp. 211–222. ACM (2014). https://doi.org/10.1145/2642937.2642980
15. Di Nitto, E., Matthews, P., Petcu, D., Solberg, A.: Model-Driven Development and Operation of Multi-Cloud Applications: The MODAClouds Approach. Springer, Cham (2017)
16. Docker Inc.: Compose Object. http://github.com/docker/compose-on-kubernetes (2020)

17. Endres, C., Breitenbücher, U., Falkenthal, M., Kopp, O., Leymann, F., Wettinger, J.: Declarative vs. imperative: two modeling patterns for the automated deployment of applications. In: Proceedings of the 9th International Conference on Pervasive Patterns and Applications, pp. 22–27. Proceedings of the 9th International Conference on Pervasive Patterns and Applications, Xpert Publishing Services (2017)
18. Farshidi, S., Jansen, S., de Jong, R., Brinkkemper, S.: A decision support system for cloud service provider selection problem in software producing organizations. In: 2018 IEEE 20th Conference on Business Informatics, vol. 01, pp. 139–148. 2018 IEEE 20th Conference on Business Informatics (CBI 2018) (2018). https://doi.org/10.1109/CBI.2018.00024
19. Guerriero, M., Garriga, M., Tamburri, D.A., Palomba, F.: Adoption, support, and challenges of infrastructure-as-code: insights from industry. In: 2019 IEEE International Conference on Software Maintenance and Evolution (ICSME), pp. 580–589 (2019). https://doi.org/10.1109/ICSME.2019.00092
20. Guillén, J., Miranda, J., Murillo, J.M., Canal, C.: A service-oriented framework for developing cross cloud migratable software. J. Syst. Softw. **86**(9), 2294–2308 (2013). https://doi.org/10.1016/j.jss.2012.12.033
21. Harzenetter, L., Breitenbücher, U., Falkenthal, M., Guth, J., Krieger, C., Leymann, F.: Pattern-based deployment models and their automatic execution. In: 11th IEEE/ACM International Conference on Utility and Cloud Computing (UCC 2018), pp. 41–52. IEEE (2018). https://doi.org/10.1109/UCC.2018.00013
22. Harzenetter, L., Breitenbücher, U., Falkenthal, M., Guth, J., Leymann, F.: Pattern-based deployment models revisited: automated pattern-driven deployment configuration. In: Proceedings of the Twelfth International Conference on Pervasive Patterns and Applications (PATTERNS 2020), pp. 40–49. Xpert Publishing Services (2020)
23. Herry, H., Anderson, P., Wickler, G.: Automated planning for configuration changes. In: Proceedings of the 25th International Conference on Large Installation System Administration, pp. 57–68. Proceedings of the 25th International Conference on Large Installation System Administration, USENIX (2011)
24. Humble, J., Farley, D.: Continuous Delivery: Reliable Software Releases Through Build, Test, and Deployment Automation. Addison-Wesley, Boston (2010)
25. Kamateri, E., et al.: Cloud4SOA: a semantic-interoperability PaaS solution for multi-cloud platform management and portability. In: Lau, K.-K., Lamersdorf, W., Pimentel, E. (eds.) ESOCC 2013. LNCS, vol. 8135, pp. 64–78. Springer, Heidelberg (2013). https://doi.org/10.1007/978-3-642-40651-5_6
26. Khajeh-Hosseini, A., Greenwood, D., Smith, J.W., Sommerville, I.: The cloud adoption toolkit: supporting cloud adoption decisions in the enterprise. Softw.: Pract. Exp. **42**(4), 447–465 (2012). https://doi.org/10.1002/spe.1072
27. Kirschnick, J., et al.: Towards an architecture for deploying elastic services in the cloud. Softw.: Pract. Exp. **42**(4), 395–408 (2012). https://doi.org/10.1002/spe.1090
28. Kopp, O., Binz, T., Breitenbücher, U., Leymann, F.: Winery – a modeling tool for TOSCA-based cloud applications. In: Basu, S., Pautasso, C., Zhang, L., Fu, X. (eds.) ICSOC 2013. LNCS, vol. 8274, pp. 700–704. Springer, Heidelberg (2013). https://doi.org/10.1007/978-3-642-45005-1_64
29. Microsoft and Alibaba Cloud: Open Application Model. http://oam.dev (2020)
30. Morris, K.: Infrastructure as Code: Managing Servers in the Cloud, 1st edn. O'Reilly Media, Sebastopol (2016)
31. OAM-dev: Kubevela. http://github.com/oam-dev/kubevela (2020)
32. OASIS: Topology and Orchestration Specification for Cloud Applications (TOSCA) Version 1.0. http://docs.oasis-open.org/tosca/TOSCA/v1.0/TOSCA-v1.0.html (2013)
33. OASIS: TOSCA Simple Profile in YAML Version 1.2. http://docs.oasis-open.org/tosca/TOSCA-Simple-Profile-YAML/v1.2/os/TOSCA-Simple-Profile-YAML-v1.2-os.html (2019)

34. Oppenheimer, D., Ganapathi, A., Patterson, D.A.: Why do internet services fail, and what can be done about it? In: Proceedings of the 4th Conference on USENIX Symposium on Internet Technologies and Systems. Proceedings of the 4th Conference on USENIX Symposium on Internet Technologies and Systems, USENIX (2003)
35. Panarello, A., Breitenbücher, U., Leymann, F., Puliafito, A., Zimmermann, M.: Automating the deployment of multi-cloud applications in federated cloud environments. In: Proceedings of the 10th EAI International Conference on Performance Evaluation Methodologies and Tools, pp. 194–201. Institute for Computer Sciences, Social-Informatics and Telecommunications Engineering (ICST) (2017). https://doi.org/10.4108/eai.25-10-2016.2266363
36. Papazoglou, M.P., van den Heuvel, W.J.: Blueprinting the cloud. IEEE Internet Comput. 15(6), 74–79 (2011). https://doi.org/10.1109/MIC.2011.147
37. Shahin, M., Ali Babar, M., Zhu, L.: Continuous integration, delivery and deployment: a systematic review on approaches, tools, challenges and practices. IEEE Access 5, 3909–3943 (2017). https://doi.org/10.1109/ACCESS.2017.2685629
38. Shuaib, M., Samad, A., Alam, S., Siddiqui, S.T.: Why adopting cloud is still a challenge?—a review on issues and challenges for cloud migration in organizations. In: Hu, Y.-C., Tiwari, S., Mishra, K.K., Trivedi, M.C. (eds.) Ambient Communications and Computer Systems. AISC, vol. 904, pp. 387–399. Springer, Singapore (2019). https://doi.org/10.1007/978-981-13-5934-7_35
39. Spring: Petclinic. http://github.com/spring-projects/spring-petclinic (2021)
40. The Kubenetes Authors: Kompose. http://kompose.io (2020)
41. Wettinger, J., Andrikopoulos, V., Leymann, F., Strauch, S.: Middleware-oriented deployment automation for cloud applications. IEEE Trans. Cloud Comput. 6(4), 1054–1066 (2018). https://doi.org/10.1109/TCC.2016.2535325
42. Wurster, M.: EDMM in YAML specification. http://github.com/UST-EDMM/spec-yaml (2019)
43. Wurster, M., Breitenbücher, U., Brogi, A., Diez, F., Leymann, F., Soldani, J., Wild, K.: Automating the deployment of distributed applications by combining multiple deployment technologies. In: Proceedings of the 11th International Conference on Cloud Computing and Services Science - CLOSER, pp. 178–189. INSTICC, SciTePress (2021). https://doi.org/10.5220/0010404301780189
44. Wurster, M., et al.: The EDMM modeling and transformation system. In: Yangui, S., et al. (eds.) ICSOC 2019. LNCS, vol. 12019, pp. 294–298. Springer, Cham (2020). https://doi.org/10.1007/978-3-030-45989-5_26
45. Wurster, M., et al.: Technology-agnostic declarative deployment automation of cloud applications. In: Brogi, A., Zimmermann, W., Kritikos, K. (eds.) ESOCC 2020. LNCS, vol. 12054, pp. 97–112. Springer, Cham (2020). https://doi.org/10.1007/978-3-030-44769-4_8
46. Wurster, M., et al.: The essential deployment metamodel: a systematic review of deployment automation technologies. SICS Softw.-Intensive Cyber-Phys. Syst. 1, 63–75 (2019). https://doi.org/10.1007/s00450-019-00412-x
47. Wurster, M., Breitenbücher, U., Harzenetter, L., Leymann, F., Soldani, J.: TOSCA lightning: an integrated toolchain for transforming TOSCA light into production-ready deployment technologies. In: Herbaut, N., La Rosa, M. (eds.) CAiSE 2020. LNBIP, vol. 386, pp. 138–146. Springer, Cham (2020). https://doi.org/10.1007/978-3-030-58135-0_12
48. Wurster, M., Breitenbücher, U., Harzenetter, L., Leymann, F., Soldani, J., Yussupov, V.: Tosca light: bridging the gap between the TOSCA specification and production-ready deployment technologies. In: Proceedings of the 10th International Conference on Cloud Computing and Services Science - Volume 1: CLOSER, pp. 216–226. INSTICC, SciTePress (2020). https://doi.org/10.5220/0009794302160226

Toward Secure VMs Allocation: Analysis of VMs Allocation Behaviours in the Cloud Computing Environments

Mansour Aldawood[1(✉)], Arshad Jhumka[1], and Suhaib A. Fahmy[2,3]

[1] Department of Computer Science, University of Warwick, Coventry, UK
{m.aldawood,h.a.jhumka}@warwick.ac.uk
[2] King Abdullah University of Science and Technology (KAUST), Thuwal, Saudi Arabia
suhaib.fahmy@kaust.edu.sa
[3] School of Engineering, University of Warwick, Coventry, UK

Abstract. Side-channel attacks (SCAs) is a potential threat in cloud computing environments (CCEs) as it allows the malicious VMs to capture private information from the target VMs when they share the same PM. This malicious co-residency of VMs is an outcome of the VMs allocation algorithm behaviour, which is responsible for allocating the VMs to a specific PM based on defined allocation objectives. Earlier studies tackled the SCAs, through specific solutions, by focusing on either formulating VMs allocation algorithms or modifying the architecture of the CCEs to mitigate the threats of SCAs. However, most of them are oriented to specific situations and assumptions, leading to malicious co-residency when applied to other scopes or situations. In this paper, we presented the solution from a different holistic perspective by examining the allocation behaviours of different algorithms and other properties that affect and lead to obtaining a secure VMs allocation. The examinations are performed under different scenarios and structures for each behaviour to understand the possible situations that lead to secure VMs allocation. In addition, we develop a deterministic security-aware VMs allocation algorithm that aims to allocate the VMs securely to reduce the potential threats from malicious co-residency in CCEs.

Keywords: Cloud computing · Virtual machines secure allocation · Side-channel attacks

1 Introduction

Cloud computing users can utilise the computing resources or services offered by the cloud service providers (CSPs) through the network and on-demand basis. These services include servers, storage, networks, applications and other services. The virtualisation technique is the core of cloud computing systems, where it enables the abstraction and sharing of computing resources accessible across a network by a group of users. Virtualisation enables a group of virtual machines (VMs) belonging to different users to share the physical machines (PMs) while running separately. In the traditional on-premises computing data centre, a PM will be dedicated to a single-purpose application, while in cloud computing, many applications belongings to different users can be hosted on a single PM [19].

© Springer Nature Switzerland AG 2022
D. Ferguson et al. (Eds.): CLOSER 2021, CCIS 1607, pp. 25–46, 2022.
https://doi.org/10.1007/978-3-031-21637-4_2

The virtualisation allows the CSPs to maximise the utilisation of the cloud resources while minimising the cost of operating the cloud infrastructure. Moreover, it enhances the cloud users utilisation of computing resources based on their needs to avoid resources wastage; thus, the provisioning of resources is elastic, based on user requirements. As a consequence, the physical resources are shared among users, and the security threats for the CCEs have invariably shifted as the types of threats that arise when a malicious user shares the resources with a target user [3]. In other words, VMs co-location, though enabling efficient resource sharing, is creating unwanted side channels, which can be sources of potential Side-channel attacks (SCAs), such as cache-based SCAs. This attack will have an impact extending from the application level to the hardware level and becoming more prevalent due to the range of side channels [7].

Thus, to overcome the problem of SCAs, it is crucial that malicious VMs, i.e., those wishing to steal information, and target VMs, i.e., those with sensitive information, are not co-resident on the same PM. Otherwise stated, the VMs allocation algorithm responsible for allocating the VMs into specific PMs needs to be security-oriented to defend against the SCAs threats. In general, the VMs allocation's objective depends on the desired outcome of the allocation process, for instance, reducing the power consumption of the PMs. In some cases, the allocation objective is related to network traffic control, which allocates the related VMs on the same network subnet [23]. In comparison, this paper focuses on the VMs allocation algorithms that aim to allocate the VMs securely in CCEs to defend against SCAs.

The previous researches tackling the SCAs and malicious VMs co-residency in CCEs focused on either finding a solution logically on the VMs level or physically on the PMs level. While in this paper we will investigate the behaviour of various state-of-the-art VMs allocation algorithms and their effect on producing secure VMs allocations. In our earlier work [2], we proposed the study of secure VMs allocation behaviours, however, the study was preliminary and did not cover more situations and properties that effect obtaining secure VMs allocations.

As such, the following points summarise the intended outcomes of this research:

1. Investigate the behaviour of various state-of-the-art VMs allocation algorithms and their effect on producing secure allocations. These are (i) Round Robin [6], (ii) Random [4] (iii) previously selected servers first (PSSF) [18] and (iv) Secure Random Stacking (SRS) [2]. Each of these algorithms has unique allocation behaviours. Hence, we consider three VMs allocation behaviours: (i) stacking, (ii) spreading and (iii) Random.
2. Develop and evaluate deterministic secure VMs allocation algorithm called Secure Stacking (SS) that aim to reduce the chance of malicious co-residency while using fewer available PMs in the cloud system.
3. Examine the effect of defined properties on producing secure VMs allocations. These properties are: (i) The impact of VMs arrival based on their type. For instance, study the impact of the arrival of malicious VMs before the target VMs. (ii) The impact of the number of VMs based on their classified type. For example, the arrival of many malicious VMs while the number of target VMs is small. (iii) The impact of the structure of the available resources of the PMs or demanded resources of the VMs. (iv) The impact of the VMs allocation behaviours algorithms on the VMs

migration number and PMs usage. In other words, studying the effect of the number of VMs migrated and the number of PMs utilised during the allocation will aim to achieve secure VMs allocation.

Generally, the extensive examination of the allocations behaviours under different properties shows that the stacking-based behaviours algorithms are more likely to produce secure allocations than those with spreading-based or random-based allocation behaviours algorithms. As such, our stacking-based algorithm are significantly better as they produce secure allocations more than the compared algorithms under the same examined situations. Furthermore, our results show that VMs arrival time has a considerable impact on the secure allocations, where the arrival of target or malicious VMs earlier than the rest of VMs often leads to malicious co-residency avoidance. Lastly, our stacking-based algorithm show the lowest PMs usage among the compared algorithms, by significant amounts, under most examined situations, leading to utilising fewer PMs and therefore fewer power consumption of the available resources. Moreover, the number VMs migration is the lowest among the examined algorithms. Hence, leading to the high availability of the VMs in cloud systems by avoiding many interruptions resulting from the VMs migration while enhancing the state of the secure allocations.

The following sections of the paper are structured as follows; In Sect. 2, we will introduce the related works and domains tackling the SCA problem in CCEs. Subsequently, in Sect. 3, we will develop and examine the considered secure VMs allocation model in CCEs. Afterwards, in Sect. 4, we will present our secure VMs allocation algorithm. Then, in Sect. 5, we will present an extensive evaluation and comparison with other VMs allocation behaviours. Finally, in Sect. 6, we will conclude our work by summarising the key findings and propose possible future works direction.

2   Related Work

This section reviews previous researches tackling the SCAs and malicious VMs co-residency in CCEs. The areas that tackled SCAs focused on either finding a solution logically on the VMs level or physically on the PMs level. The section divides the previous research into six domains aiming to secure the VMs allocation process in CCEs from different perspectives.

The first domain focuses on grouping the VMs based on defined requirements through the VMs allocation. Then, these requirements cluster the VMs into groups to achieve secure VMs allocation. In [22], they proposed a group-based allocation policy to optimise the resources and obtain a secure VMs allocation by establishing group instances for the VMs. These groups have specific requirements such as group size limit or resource availability which defines the number of distinct users in each group, not only the number of VMs. This user size limitation potentially enhances the secure allocation of the VMs. In [9,17,21,29,30], other grouping approaches focus on isolating the allocated VMs into groups based on defined requirements such as network dependency or attributes that define VMs users.

The second domain considers another form of grouping as it depends on allocating the VMs based on either profiling the VMs or based on security compliance requirements. For example, in [10], a method was proposed to allocate the VMs by maintaining the same security standard as the co-located VMs, such as the ISO standard. Similarly, in [1,5], their scheme validates the level of security of each upcoming VMs, which must comply with specific compliance regulation. In comparison, some works focus on generalising the VMs allocation based on profiling the users and integrating the outcome with the existing placement constraints [25].

In the third domain, the solutions focus on allocating the VMs for a defined time to reduce the amount of sensitive data leakage through the SCAs. The SCAs happens when malicious VMs co-locate for a certain amount of time with target VMs, then initiate the attack by capturing related information, through the leakage channels, about the target VMs activities. Thus, these proposals focuses on reducing the amount of data leakage due to the SCAs by considering the time factor for VMs residing on specific PMs [24,27].

The fourth domain focuses on developing algorithms that manipulate the cloud system's scheduling component. For example, in [8], introduce an algorithm that deliberately delayed the start-up time for VMs to reduce the chance of co-residency with malicious VMs. While in [32], they focus on migrating the VMs frequently by using an incentive approach, by providing better PMs with more free resources to stimulate the users to migrate their VMs. Thus, to move the VMs periodically to reduce the probability of malicious co-residency. Further, in [4,18], their algorithms randomly select and allocate VMs into specific PMs to reduce the chance of co-residency.

The fifth domain follows an optimisation-based approach to secure VMs allocation while utilising existing solutions related to ideal situations. For instance, in [11], they proposed a solution that depends on utilising an optimisation-based problem called Dolphin Partner, prioritising the VMs with the most efficient energy-aware and memory-aware utilisation. Their work focuses on the parameters that potentially cause a failure for the VM, for example, the memory utilisation of the VM. Thus, if the current utilisation of a VM is high, it is more prone to failure and considered a less secure. Similarly, in [12], they proposed a solution to enhance the security and performance of the VMs allocation process using the firefly algorithm to produce an optimal secure allocation. Moreover, [16] presented a secure VMs allocation algorithm based on multi-objective optimisation by extending the First-Fit algorithm, which provides an allocation that satisfies the resource constraint.

The last domain focuses on the secure VMs allocation on the hardware level of the cloud system. The mechanism includes partitioning memory caches or CPU processing threads to defend against the software level of SCAs. It requires a modification in the hardware level, which includes either changing the mechanism of an existing components or adding new ones [14,20,31].

3   Problem Formulation

We will define the model of the secure VMs allocation in CCEs, including the definition of the model's objective and its assumed constraints. The model's objective is to obtain a secure VMs allocation to defend against SCAs by minimising the malicious co-residency. Moreover, it includes defining the objective of the VMs allocation, which is producing a secure VMs allocation under different situations while reducing the utilised PMs. In addition, we defined the threats of malicious users, including the attacker's behaviour and the impact of the attack that the SCAs could leave on the compromised system. Furthermore, we will define cloud users based on their behaviour analysis, thus, classifying them into specific types.

3.1 Threat Model

In CCEs, resource allocation is flexible and enables multiple users to share a common computing platform dynamically. When VMs are co-resident or co-located on the same PM, a malicious VM can analyse characteristics of another target VM, e.g., analysing the operations timing properties, to infer various information such as cryptographic keys through SCAs. For instance, the SCA can occur through a cache-based channel by utilising the sharing capabilities of the cache levels. In other words, the malicious VMs can analyse the execution time of the VMs co-locating on the same PM and subsequently conduct the attack. This analysis starts by capturing the execution data of the target VMs, then analysing them to formulate an attacks model using a machine learning-based approach [26].

Achieving Malicious Co-residency. From the malicious user perspective, the first step of conducting SCA is to achieve a co-residency with the target VMs, leading to a malicious co-residency. Achieving such a goal depends on the VMs allocation algorithm that the CSP utilises to allocate the VMs. Alternatively stated, the behaviour of the VMs allocation algorithm contributes significantly to achieving malicious co-residency by the malicious VM. Therefore, the malicious user needs to understand how the CSPs allocates the VMs to formulate the attacks based on this knowledge. For instance, in [28], they studied the possibility of achieving a malicious co-residency based on the allocation algorithms on different public CCEs, such as Amazon or Google. Their study concluded that the malicious user could reach this goal simply and cheaply due to the vulnerabilities of the VMs allocation algorithms. Hence, the malicious co-residency can be achieved due to the limitation of the allocation algorithms not considering the severity and impact.

Capturing Execution Time Data. After the malicious co-residency occurs between the malicious VMs and the target VMs, the malicious user will initiate the SCA. In this work, we assumed the cache-based attack as the considered attack model conducted by the malicious user. It starts by utilising the vulnerabilities of the shared cache among VMs allocated on the same PM. The malicious VMs can perform the attack by measuring the execution time of the load operations of the shared caches on the PM level. If a specific operation utilises a considerable amount of time to load, compared to the other operations, the attacker will deduce a current encrypted operation executing on the physical machine from a co-resided VM [7].

Overall, the SCAs collect information from normal operations output, such as execution time on cache levels. Furthermore, the collected information has no major impacts when treated separately. However, with sophisticated tools that can classify and cluster irrelevant data to meaningful information, such as machine learning tools, this process can lead to major SCAs. Otherwise stated, the extracted information will help to profile the activities of the VMs co-located on the same PM and define the vulnerable state of the target VMs. For example, in [15], they utilise a machine learning-based approach to conduct a cache-based attack by profiling the activities of cloud users. They captured data features resulting from cache-based access that represents different types of applications. Their approach showed that the captured information could be collected regardless of synchronising the cache access between the malicious and target VMs.

3.2 Secure VMs Allocation Model

The main objective of the proposed secure VMs allocation model is to obtain a secure allocation where the target VMs and malicious VMs not sharing the same PM, thus, defending against SCAs. Moreover, the proposed model aims to find allocations where the number of used PMs is minimised. Therefore, our model following a stacking-based VMs allocation behaviour such as Bin-Packing problem (BPP) [13].

Definition of Variables and Functions. The following are the variables and functions definitions of the model:

1. $P = PM_1 \ldots PM_k$: *Set of physical machines.*
2. $R(PM_j)$: *Available resources of a physical machine (j).*
3. $V = VM^1 \ldots VM^n$: *Set of virtual machines.*
4. $N(VM^i)$: *Required resources of a virtual machine (i).*
5. T: *Set of virtual machines classified as a Target.*
6. M: *Set of virtual machines classified as a Malicious.*
7. N: *Set of virtual machines classified as a Normal.*
8. $A_u : V \rightarrow P$: *VM allocation function to a PM.*
9. $Move(A_u, A_{u+1})$: *Set of VMs that are migrated during transition from (A_u) to (A_{u+1}).*
10. $CoRe(A_u)$: *Set of PMs at which malicious co-residency occurs.*

Objective Function Formulation. In summation, we will define the objective function and its constraints of the proposed model as an approximation of BPP. Our main objective is to obtain a secure VMs allocation while reducing the number of used PMs. In other words, the priority is not reducing the utilised PMs, the priority to obtain a secure VMs allocation; however, it is a constraint to influence the allocation algorithm if it is only possible while maintaining secure allocations. Thus, our objective function is described as follow:

The objective is *Minimize*

$$\sum_{i=1}^{n} CoRe(A_u) * x_{ij} \qquad \forall_{i \in V,\, j \in P,\, \text{for}(j=1\ldots k)} \tag{1}$$

Subject to:

$$\sum_{j=1}^{k} y_j \leq |P| \qquad \forall_{j \in P} \tag{2}$$

$$\sum_{i=1}^{n} N(VM^i) * x_{ij} \leq R(PM_j) * y_j \qquad \forall_{i \in V, \, j \in P, \, \text{for}(j=1...k)} \tag{3}$$

$$\sum_{i=1}^{n} x_{ij} = 1 \qquad \forall_{i \in V, \, j \in P, \, \text{for}(j=1...k)} \tag{4}$$

$$x_{ij} \in \{0,1\}, \qquad \forall_{\text{for}(i=1...n), \, \text{for}(j=1...k)} \tag{5}$$

$$y_j \in \{0,1\}, \qquad \forall_{\text{for}(j=1...k)} \tag{6}$$

Starting from Eq. (1), which aims to minimise the malicious co-residency of a selected possible allocation, i.e., for each possible VMs allocation of requested VMs and available PMs, the objective is to select a possible allocation that yields to produce an allocation with minimum malicious co-residency. The first constraint in Eq. (2) is to make sure that the selected number of PMs is reduced as much as possible. As we stated earlier, we aim to allocate the VMs into selected PMs while minimising the used PMs as an objective, but in our model, we utilised this objective as a constraint. Because our goal is to obtain a secure VMs allocation while reducing the number of used PMs as much as possible. The second constraint in Eq. (3) will verify that the requested resources of the selected VMs are not exceeding the available resources of the available PMs. The third one, in Eq. (4), verifies that each VM is allocated once on a single PM to prevent duplicated allocations. The equations, Eq. (5 to 6) are defining the decisions variables needed for selecting the best possible allocations, which are x_{ij} and y_j. The x_{ij} responsible for selecting the best allocation that results in obtaining a minimum malicious co-residency. The x_{ij} is an integer value of either 0 or 1, where one means the allocation is selected and zero otherwise. The y_j responsible for selecting the allocations with fewer possible numbers of PMs.

VMs Migration. In case a VM migration triggered, we formulate the following equation as a constraint of the objective function:

$$|Move(A_u, A_{u+1})| \leq \beta \tag{7}$$

This equation denotes that the number of VMs in a set of VMs that are selected for a VM migration, $Move(A_u, A_{u+1})$, is less than or equal to a defined threshold, β. In other words, for each transition from A_u to A_{u+1}, the number of VMs selected, for migration, should not exceed a certain defined threshold. Defining the threshold depends on several aspects that determine how many VMs can be selected, such as an service level agreement (SLA) that forces some VMs to be allocated on a PM at all times. In this case, these VMs will not be selected for VMs migration even if they are eligible; therefore, the number of VMs migrating is reduced.

VMs Learning Model. As stated in our earlier work [2], we introduce a learning module which aims to classify the VMs based on their behaviours. The analysis of VMs behaviour is crucial for CSPs to identify VMs with suspicious behaviour and isolate them from other VMs. Briefly, the analysis of the learning model produces a categorisation of the VMs into three types; these types are target, malicious and normal VMs. Formally stated, the set V, the set of all VMs available in CCEs, is partitioned into three sets: (i) set T of target VMs, (ii) set M of malicious VMs and (iii) set N of normal VMs.

4   Secure VMs Allocation Algorithm

We propose a deterministic security-aware heuristic, a variant of bin-packing, called Secure Stacking (SS), which is shown in Algorithm 1. Mainly, SS aims to allocate VMs in a stacking fashion and migrates them from one PM to another if the possibility of VM migration exists. Like a BPP, the SS algorithm aims to allocate the VMs into the selected PMs while using a smaller number of available PMs and to maintain a secure allocation. The motivation behind utilising a smaller number of PMs is to avoid VMs migration during the allocation, which leads to unwanted service interruptions of the VMs during the migration process.

4.1   Secure Stacking Algorithm (SS)

The SS algorithm has two main inputs: (i) the unallocated set of VMs, denoted as **V** and (ii) the set of the available PMs, denoted as **P**. The output, denoted as the **A**, is the secure allocation produced for the available set of resources.

The SS algorithm starts, at line 3, by allocating the VMs, in the set of unallocated VMs in the set of the available PMs. It goes through three trials of allocating the VMs, and each trial has its specific functions. From line 5 to line 10, the first try aims to allocate the VMs securely in a stacking fashion without triggering the VMs migration. Meaning the SS will try to obtain a secure VMs allocation while meeting the required resources constraints without changing the structure of the current VMs allocation, i.e., triggering VMs migrations. On the second try, from line 11 to line 15, the SS will try again to obtain a secure VM allocation for the same VM; however, this time will trigger the VM migrations, thus changing the current structure of the allocated VMs. On the third try, from line 16 to line 23, the SS reach the point to allocate the VM to any available PM, regardless of the security constraints. Meaning the priority at this point is to obtain a VM allocation to any suitable PM.

Fullness Ratio. In line 4, the SS will sort the available PMs based on their fullness ratio (FR) by comparing the require resources of the VM, denoted as v, with the available PMs resources. In other words, the SS prioritised the PMs for an allocation based on the fullness of each PM, which means that each PM will be filled differently after the allocation of the upcoming VM. Thus, triggering *getSortedFRPMs(v, P)* that compares each requires resource from the VM (v) to the available PMs resources. Then, we will sort the PMs based on the FR and produce a list of the sorted PMs, called *sortedPMsList*.

Algorithm 1. Secure Stacking (SS) VMs Allocation.

Input: V: Set of unallocated VMs, **P**: Set of PMs
Output: A: Secure Allocation

1 sortedPMsList ← ∅
2 COR ← *Flase*
3 **for** *v in V* **do**
4 | sortedPMsList ← getSortedFRPMs(v,P)
   | // First try to allocate v
5 | **for** *p in sortedPMs* **do**
6 | | COR ← getCORvmCheck(v,p.getVMslist())
7 | | **if** *COR ≠ True* **then**
8 | | | A ← Assign(v,p)
9 | | **end**
10 | **end**
11 | **if** *v.getPM() = ∅* // Second try, migrate VMs then retry
   | allocate v
12 | **then**
13 | | vmMigration(sortedPMsList,P)
14 | | Repeat steps from 5–10
15 | **end**
16 | **if** *v.getPM() = ∅* // Third try, allocate v in any available *P*
17 | **then**
18 | | **for** *p in P* **do**
19 | | | **if** *p.suitablePM(v) = True* **then**
20 | | | | A ← Assign(v,p)
21 | | | **end**
22 | | **end**
23 | **end**
24 **end**
25 **return A**

The main objective of the FR function, denoted as *getSortedFRPMs(v,P)*, is to sort the available PMs resources according to their FR compares to the VM required resources that needs to be allocated. Therefore, the FR function is comparing the remaining resources of each PM with demanded resources of the upcoming VM. This comparison results in a sorted PMs list based on how much the PM will be filled after the allocation if the allocation occurs. Hence the SS algorithm following a stacking-based behaviour in allocating the VMs. We consider the RAM size and the CPU cores with their sizes are the essential resources to be validated during the FR calculation. Thus, we will explain how the calculation of the FR for the multidimensional resources (MR) is performed in the FR function

The detailed calculation of MR described as follow:

$$MR = (VM_{ram} \div PM_{ram}) + (VM_{cpu} \div PM_{cpu}) \qquad (8)$$

The idea is to compare the VM with the PM, considering the RAM and CPU specifications. In Eq. (8), firstly, the FR function divides the required RAM of the VM by the available RAM of the PM. If the results of this part are exceeding one, then it means that the required RAM is more than the available RAM of PM; thus, this PM is discarded. Then, repeat the same division of the RAM part with the CPU part. Moreover, finally sum the result of the two parts, the RAM and CPU calculation. If the result is equal to two, then this PM is a perfect match for the VM. In other words, this PM will be the first PM selected for possible allocation. The results represent how much the PM will be utilised for the unallocated VM; thus, it will be prioritised based on this result.

First Try. We will start with the first try and explain its main functions, from lines 5 to 10. In line 5, the SS will try the first PM, denoted as p, out of the produced FR PMs to allocate the unallocated VM on it, denoted as v. The p, at this stage, represent the highest FR of the available PMs. Meaning, this p, if selected, will yield to be filled more than the other available PMs. Thus, this step is contributing to the stacking behaviour of the SS allocation algorithm. Then, in line 6, the SS will check if allocating the VM, v, yields a malicious co-residency. According to the presented learning model, in [2], each VM in the CCEs classified into either target, malicious or normal VM. Thus, at this step, the SS will compare the upcoming VM with the allocated VMs on the selected PM, if any, for malicious co-residency. If the malicious co-residency will occurs after allocating the VM, this PM will be discarded from the allocation and moved on to the following PM. The result of this checking is preserved in a Boolean variable denoted as COR after triggering the $getCORvmCheck(v,p.getVMslist())$ function. This function is essential to the SS as it will be the main responsible for triggering the VMs migration in the second try. The last step of the first try, in line 8, is to assign the v into the selected p if previous conditions are met.

Second Try. In lines 11 to 15, the second try starts if the first try failed to obtain a secure allocation for the unallocated VM. As indicated in line 11, the second try is triggered if the v is not allocated to a PM yet. The primary step of this try, in line 13, is the VM migration function, which is changing the structure of the current VMs allocation by moving the allocated VMs, if possible, to another PMs to obtain a secure VM allocation. The VMs migration aims to migrate a few VMs to obtain a secure allocation for the unallocated VM and enhance, or keep, the current secure allocation state. In other words, we aim to migrate the VMs while reducing the number of VMs migrated and maximising, or maintaining, the current security state of allocated VMs.

The $vmMigration(sortedPMsList, P)$ receives the list PMs to select their VMs for migration and the available PMs set, to select the destination PM after migration. The selection step, selecting the PMs list, aims to select the minimum number of VMs for migration, thus reducing the VM movements. For example, the SS algorithm utilises the VMs migration function by sending the list of the sorted PMs, to migrate their VMs. This list of PMs has a low number of VMs compared to all the available PMs. Thus, the VMs allocated on these VMs will be minimal; hence the VMs selected for migration will be minimised. We consider this way of selecting the VMs for migration to allow few effective migrations that potentially leads to a more secure allocation and fewer VMs interruptions resulted from the migration. Although the number of VMs selected for migration will be higher at some point in time, specifically when there is a high number of PMs available with high (FR%).

Third Try. The last step of the SS algorithm is started, in lines 16 to 23, if the previous two steps failed to obtain a secure VM allocation. At this step, the SS will allocate v to any available PM regardless of the malicious co-residency allocation constraints. In other words, as long as the selected PM has enough available resources, it will be selected to host the unallocated VM. Afterwards, in line 25, all the assignments will be registered in **A** and returned as a final allocation.

5   Evaluation

We will present a detailed evaluation of the proposed algorithms under different PMs and VMs structures and different allocation scenarios. As such, we study the effect of VMs allocation behaviour on obtaining a secure allocations. The behaviours are stacking, spreading and random behaviour. We investigate the factors affecting the outcome towards obtaining a secure allocation. These are; the PMs heterogeneity level, the diversity of available resources, the VMs arrival time for each type of VMs considered in this work and the number of VMs according to their classified type. Additionally, we study the effect of VMs migration and the efficient PMs usage for the proposed algorithms on the overall outcome of a secure allocation.

5.1   Allocation Behaviours Comparison

In this part, we will introduce the VMs allocation behaviours algorithms to compare our SS algorithm with them, and each of them has a unique allocation behaviour. The first one is spreading behaviour, which means that the allocation algorithm will allocate VMs to the whole span of PMs. An example of the spreading behaviour is the round-robin algorithm, denoted as RR, described in [6]. The second one is random behaviour (Random), which aims to allocate the VMs randomly as long as the candidate PM is suitable. In [4], they presented a random-based algorithm aiming to allocate the VMs randomly. The third considered allocation behaviour, called the PSSF, is a combination of spreading and random behaviour. This behaviour algorithm, described in [18], depends on spreading the VMs of the same user if they exceeded three VMs on the same PM and, eligible PMs are selected randomly if they have less than three VMs of the same user. Moreover, we include our previous algorithm, SRS, in the comparison of this work [2].

Furthermore, we modify the three algorithms, RR, Random and PSSF, by making them aware of the learning model outcome. Otherwise stated, we have added the co-residency detection function while keeping their allocation behaviour the same. These algorithms will allocate the VMs as they have been doing unless there is a malicious co-residency in the allocation.

5.2   Experimental Setup

We will explain the simulation environment utilised in this work, the structure of the PMs resources considered during the allocation process, the VMs structure including the VMs arrival times and the structure of VMs type.

Simulation Environment. Similar to our earlier work [2], we utilise CloudSim, a cloud computing simulation environment, to examine the proposed VMs allocation algorithms and compare them.

VMs and PMs Number. The VMs range from 20–120, increasing by 20 VMs in each experiment. The number of PMs is 24 in each experiment, where the sum of available resources of the PMs can accommodate up to 120 VMs. Thus, the experiments will start by allocating the VMs with vast available resources; then, the resources get limited until it reaches 120 VMs. The resource requirements of the VMs are similar with 1 GB vRAM (Virtual RAM), 1 vCPU and 500 MB vStorage. On the other hand, the resources available for each PM are heterogeneous. There are four types of PMs used for this setup: (i) 2 GB RAM and 2 CPU, (ii) 4 GB RAM and 4 CPU, (iii) 6 GB RAM and 6 CPU, and (iv) 8 GB RAM and 8 CPU.

VMs Arrival Time. We consider three arrival times (launch times), to show the effect of VMs arrival time, based on its type, on the malicious co-residency. The three arrival times are $M(t)$, $T(t)$ and $N(t)$. The $M(t)$ is the time that the malicious VM is arrived. The same definition applies to $T(t)$ and $N(t)$ for target VM and normal VM, respectively.

Table 1. VMs arrival time types.

Tries no.	VMs order	Description
1	GNMT	G(N), G(M), G(T)
2	SNMT	S(N), S(M), S(T)
3	Mixed NMT	S(NMT), G(N), S(NMT), G(M), S(NMT), G(T), S(NMT)

As shown in Table 1, we study some of the possibilities of VMs arrival time based on each type of VMs. For instance, in try 1, we study when a group of normal VMs arrives, then a group of malicious VMs arrives, then a group of target VMs arrives last, denoted as GNMT. Furthermore, in try 2, the VMs will arrive a single instead of a group, meaning one normal VM arrives, followed by malicious, followed by target, denoted as SNMT. Lastly, in the try 3, we study the arrival time as a mixed of single and group arrivals. The size of each group, the seven groups of the mixed order type, divided equally to each group. The motivation behind designing the arrival times in this sequence is to mimic the real-world scenario of VMs arrival as much as possible.

VMs Type Structure. Table 2 considers seven possible situations where each VMs type number might reach for each experiment. Moreover, each VMs type number, tries 1 for instance, will be examined for its secure VMs allocation level and how it performs under this defined configuration. To explain, if we consider 20 VMs, then this VMs type number will be structured 7 times, as described in Table 2, and examined for each situation. The seven tries are because we have three VMs types considered, and $2^3 = 8$ possible situations. However, we discarded the one where the VMs type number are zeros from these eight possible situations.

Table 2. VMs type structure.

Tries no.	% Malicious VMs	%Normal VMs	%Target VMs
1	25	25	50
2	25	50	25
3	26	37	37
4	50	25	25
5	37	26	37
6	37	37	26
7	33	34	33

PMs Heterogeneity Levels. We consider three types of PMs structure, or level of PMs heterogeneity, High, Medium and Low heterogeneous PMs. Meaning the resources of the PMs are structured based on the classification of PMs heterogeneity, as explained in [2].

5.3 Results of Malicious Co-residency Respect to VMs Type and Under Limited Resources Availability

Continue to our work in [2], we will have a closer look at the M_{pms} concerning the VMs type number, the VMs arrival and PMs heterogeneity. Here, we only will show the results when the resources are limited, which means when the number of VMs equal 120 VMs. The M_{pms} is the percentage of PMs with malicious co-residency, calculated as follow:

$$M_{pms} = \frac{I_{pms}}{U_{pms}} \tag{9}$$

where the (I_{pms}) specify the infected used PMs, and the (U_{pms}) specify the total used PMs for an allocation. We only will show the results when the resources are limited, which means when the number of VMs equal 120 VMs.

Malicious Co-residency for Group VMs Arrival Under Limited Resources. In Fig. 1, this case considers the most challenging case for any allocation algorithm, as the target and malicious VMs arrives at the end when most of the resources are already utilised.

From VMs type number perspective, the PSSF algorithm often suffers from high M_{pms} when the number of malicious VMs or targets VMs higher than the other types. In some cases, the higher number of malicious and target VMs leads to a high M_{pms}. This outcome is because this case considers the group VMs arrivals, meaning a group of VMs, possibly belonging to the same user, will be allocated simultaneously. Since the PSSF spreads the VMs of the same user, and if the user is a malicious one, then the chance of malicious co-residency occurring is very high for such allocation behaviour. The same applies when many VMs belong to a target user or arrive simultaneously

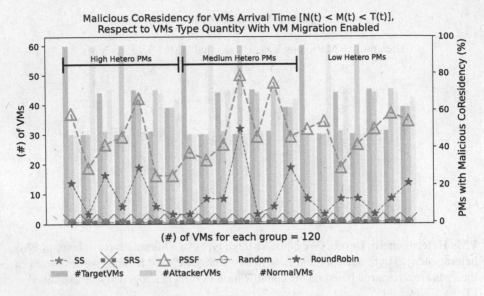

Fig. 1. Malicious co-residency under GNMT arrival time, when available resources limited.

with a considerably high number of VMs. For RR, spreading the VMs is negatively impacting the M_{pms} as it is considered among the worst of compared algorithms. The reason for the high M_{pms} is the same as we described in the PSSF algorithm, as they share the spreading behaviour of allocating the VMs. Overall, the SS, SRS, and Random algorithms are best when the VMs arrive in groups. The stacking of the VMs reduces the number of used PMs during the allocation and creates a perfect match between the required resources and the available recourse, which is what SS and SRS perform. Thus, avoiding the chance of producing allocations with high M_{pms}.

From VMs arrival time perspective, the constraint of the PSSF algorithm that keeps only three users on the same PM leads to spread target and malicious VMs, which results in higher M_{pms}. Thus, if the malicious user launched many VMs, it will be easier to obtain a malicious co-residency with the target user. Also, because the normal VMs, for each experiment, arrives first and spread their VMs on the available PMs. Hence, fewer available PMs when the malicious and target VMs arrives, which is also applies to RR algorithm.

From PMs heterogeneity perspective, when comparing the effect of PMs heterogeneity level, the low heterogeneous PMs structure often leads to a better result of M_{pms} than the other PMs structure for PSSF and RR.

Malicious Co-residency for Single VMs Arrival Under Limited Resources. In Fig. 2, the single VMs arrivals lead to better results comparing to the group or mixed VMs arrivals.

The effect of the VMs number, according to their type, is similar to the group arrivals, for all the algorithms. Briefly, the higher number of either malicious or target VMs, and in some cases when both are high, leads to a higher chance of malicious co-residency occurrence.

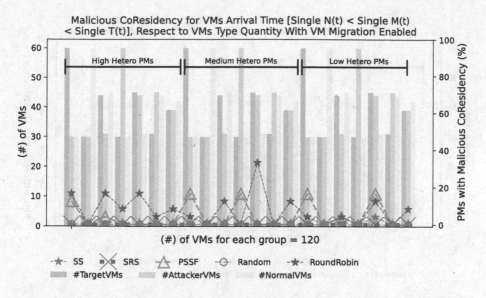

Fig. 2. Malicious co-residency under SNMT arrival time, when available resources limited.

Moreover, when the VMs arrived separately, the M_{pms} decreases significantly for the compared algorithms even when the available recourse is limited. This outcome happens because it is easier for the allocator to obtain a secure allocation for a single VM, according to its type. However, when a group of VMs of the same type arrives, it is not easy to produce a secure allocation. For example, when a group of target VMs arrives and the malicious VMs already allocated to most of the available PMs, it will be challenging for the algorithms to obtain a secure allocation, especially if the algorithm follows a spreading behaviour. On the other hand, a single target VM arriving makes it easier to obtain the secure allocation because the available PMs options that lead to secure allocation is potentially higher, even for the spreading based algorithms.

The high heterogeneous PMs structure often leads to a better result of M_{pms} than the other PMs structure for all algorithms due to the high diversity of the structure of the resources. Ultimately, the impact of VMs number continues to be the same on the single VMs arrival.

Malicious Co-residency for Mixed VMs Arrival Under Limited Resources. In Fig. 3, the outcomes of the M_{pms} is better than the group VMs arrival as this type mixed the group with the single VMs arrivals. Thus the single VMs arrival influences the positive impact of obtaining more secure allocations for all the algorithms.

From VMs type number perspective, the PSSF and Random algorithms are showing a clear relationship between the spike number of either target or malicious VMs with the high M_{pms}. Even in the cases where they both have a relatively high number at the same time compared to the total number of VMs, of the experiment. Also, the high number of normal VMs positively leads to low, sometimes none, malicious co-residency. However, this effect disappears when the number of either target or malicious VMs rises. Similarly, the RR algorithm was impacted by the rising number of

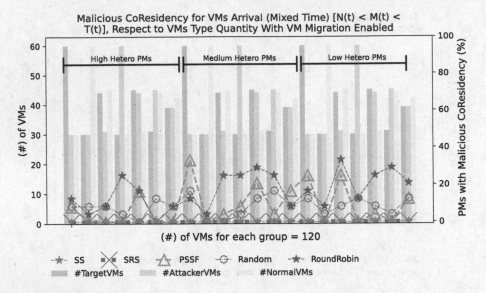

Fig. 3. Malicious co-residency under mixed NMT arrival time, when available resources limited.

target and malicious VMs. The SS and SRS continue to produce the best outcome of the compared algorithms over the examined situations.

From VMs arrival perspective, the normal VMs will arrive first, then any VM from the other two types can be allocated with them. Thus, leaving more options and more available PMs for the upcoming VMs when it arrives to obtain secure allocations. However, the single VMs arrival between the groups causing the spike of M_{pms} the same way happened in the previous arrivals.

Furthermore, PMs heterogeneous structure's effect did not seem to have that great difference between the three types in the matter of the number of spikes; however, the high heterogeneous is slightly better in most cases in the matter of producing low M_{pms}.

5.4 Results of VMs Migrations

This section will compare the result of VMs migration for all the compared algorithms under different arrival times. The percentage of VMs migrations, denoted as (Mig_{vms}), is defined as follow:

$$Mig_{vms} = \frac{S_{vms}}{T_{vms}} \tag{10}$$

where the (S_{vms}) specify the VMs selected and migrated from one PM to another, and the (T_{vms}) specify the total VMs for an allocation.

VMs Migrations for Group VMs Arrival. In general, as shown in Fig. 4, the spreading allocation behaviours algorithms, RR and PSSF, are the worst in Mig_{vms}, especially when the resources are limited. While the random algorithm, have a moderated percentage of VMs migration considering benefits produced by these migrations, which is a lower chance of malicious co-residency. The stacking-based algorithms, SS and SRS,

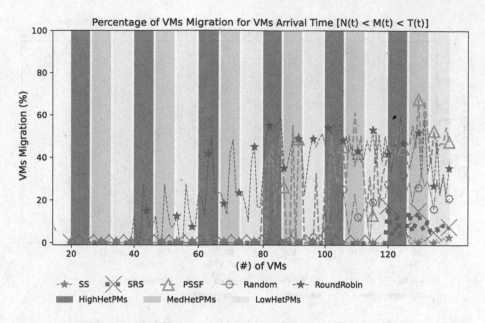

Fig. 4. VMs migrations under single VMs arrival, GNMT arrival time.

show the lowest percentage of VMs migration among the other algorithms under all the group VMs arrival. However, the SRS algorithm shows high Mig_{vms} compared to the SS algorithm in a few cases when the resources are limited and the malicious and target VMs arrive at last. The SS algorithm is considered to have the best outcome of Mig_{vms} under all the examined situations. On the other hand, the reason that influences the Mig_{vms} to be low in some cases is the limited options of the available PMs and the limited number of selected VMs for migration. As a consequence of this behaviour, the M_{pms} will produce a higher percentage than other cases of the same algorithm under different arrival times.

Overall, from the algorithm perspective, the benefits for VMs migration are high for the random, SRS and SS algorithms, but for PSSF and RR, the benefits are not significant. For instance, the high Mig_{vms} for the SRS algorithm leads to obtaining secure allocations for all the cases examined. Also, the random algorithms benefit greatly from the VMs migration as it produces many allocations without high M_{pms}. On the other hand, for RR and PSSF, their benefits are not as much as the other algorithms due to their spreading behaviour that limits VMs migration options.

VMs Migrations for Single VMs Arrival. In Fig. 5, the RR case shows high Mig_{vms} compared to the other algorithms, even when the resources are not limiting. The reason for this behaviour back to two main points; the configurations of VMs arrivals and the behaviour of the algorithm. The VMs arrival structure, in this case, depends on separating the VMs as single based on their type classification. Thus, it is easier for the malicious VMs, or target VMs, to spread access to the entire available PMs at early stages. This spreading brings us to the second reason, which is the behaviour of the algorithm, which depends on spreading the VMs upon their arrivals. Hence, making the Mig_{vms} much higher compare to the other algorithms.

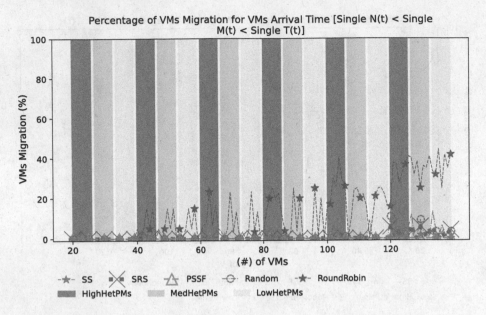

Fig. 5. VMs Migrations under single VMs arrival, SNMT arrival time.

VMs Migrations for Mixed VMs Arrival. In Fig. 6, the similarity of outcome for VMs migration continues for this type of VMs arrival, where the RR algorithm performs the worse among the compared algorithms due to its spreading behaviour. Similarly, the PSSF shows a high Mig_{vms} only when the resources start limiting, which indicates that obtaining secure allocation at this stage is challenging. Moreover, the Rand algorithm low Mig_{vms} compare to the spreading behaviour algorithms, RR and PSSF. The stacking-based algorithms, SS and SRS, are the best in this time arrivals are they yielding to the lowest Mig_{vms} for all the cases.

5.5 Results of PMs Usage

This section aims to examine the PMs utilisation, ($Usage_{pms}$), during the VMs allocations for all the compared algorithms. The PMs utilisation is also considered an indication of the power consumption for the compared algorithms. We calculate the percentage of used PMs compared to the total available PMs, denoted as ($Usage_{pms}$), as follow:

$$Usage_{pms} = \frac{U_{pms}}{T_{pms}} \tag{11}$$

where the (U_{pms}) specify the used PMs for completing an allocation, and the (T_{pms}) specify the total available PMs.

VMs Arrival (GNMT). To avoid duplication of similar results, we will only show the case of group VMs arrival, as shown in Fig. 7.

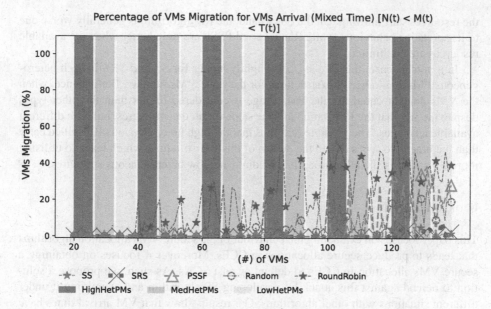

Fig. 6. VMs migrations under single VMs arrival, mixed NMT arrival time.

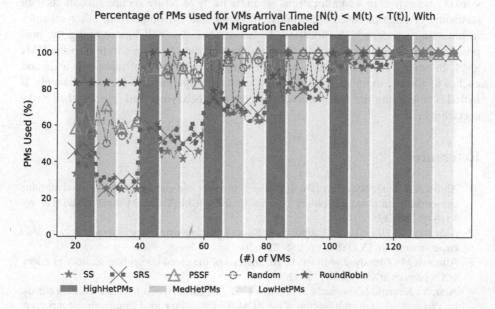

Fig. 7. PMs usage under GNMT arrival time.

Overall, in Fig. 7, there is an indication of the resource usage, efficiency towards obtaining a secure allocation. In other words, in our proposed SS algorithm, the $Usage_{pms}$ are the best among the compared algorithms under most cases, even when the resources start limiting. On the other hand, the RR algorithm is generally worse due to its spreading behaviour, while Random and PSSF are only better when the available resources are not limited.

In a notable case, the $Usage_{pms}$ is slightly higher for SS and SRS in high heterogeneous PMs than other PMs structures for the same VMs number. For instance, when the VMs number equal 20, the PMs usage is considered higher than the other types despite the fact that the PMs number is the same for all the structures, but with different available resources. The possible reason is that the high heterogeneous PMs filled early than the other two types due to the design of this PM structure, which leads to utilising more PMs, during the allocation, than medium and low heterogeneous structures.

6   Conclusion

This paper focuses on evaluating the behaviour of the secure VMs allocation algorithms that leads to produce secure allocations in CCEs. Moreover it focuses on obtaining a secure VMs allocation in CCEs to defend against SCAs. As such, we propose a solution to defend against this attack by developing SS algorithm and examining it under different situations with other algorithms. Our results show that VM arrival times have a significant impact on obtaining a secure allocation. Also, the algorithms that follow a stacking behaviour in VM allocations are more likely to return secure allocations than spreading or random-based algorithms. We show that SS outperform other schemes in obtaining a secure VM allocation. In future work, we will be extending the proposed model to include tasks allocation on the hardware level in addition to the VMs level. In other words, it depends on controlling the allocation of tasks on CPUs and caches to allocate them securely and reduce data leakage through the side channels. It includes classifying the tasks according to the user behaviour and allocate their tasks accordingly.

References

1. Ahamed, F., Shahrestani, S., Javadi, B.: Security aware and energy-efficient virtual machine consolidation in cloud computing systems. In: 2016 IEEE Trustcom/BigDataSE/ISPA, pp. 1516–1523. IEEE (2016)
2. Aldawood, M., Jhumka, A., Fahmy, S.A.: Sit here: placing virtual machines securely in cloud environments. In: CLOSER, pp. 248–259 (2021)
3. Almorsy, M., Grundy, J., Müller, I.: An analysis of the cloud computing security problem. arXiv preprint arXiv:1609.01107 (2016)
4. Azar, Y., Kamara, S., Menache, I., Raykova, M., Shepard, B.: Co-location-resistant clouds. In: Proceedings of the 6th Edition of the ACM Workshop on Cloud Computing Security, pp. 9–20 (2014)
5. Bahrami, M., Malvankar, A., Budhraja, K.K., Kundu, C., Singhal, M., Kundu, A.: Compliance-aware provisioning of containers on cloud. In: 2017 IEEE 10th International Conference on Cloud Computing (CLOUD), pp. 696–700. IEEE (2017)
6. Balharith, T., Alhaidari, F.: Round robin scheduling algorithm in CPU and cloud computing: a review. In: 2019 2nd International Conference on Computer Applications and Information Security (ICCAIS), pp. 1–7. IEEE (2019)

7. Bazm, M.M., Lacoste, M., Südholt, M., Menaud, J.M.: Side channels in the cloud: isolation challenges, attacks, and countermeasures (2017)

8. Berrima, M., Nasr, A.K., Ben Rajeb, N.: Co-location resistant strategy with full resources optimization. In: Proceedings of the 2016 ACM on Cloud Computing Security Workshop, pp. 3–10 (2016)

9. Bijon, K., Krishnan, R., Sandhu, R.: Mitigating multi-tenancy risks in IAAS cloud through constraints-driven virtual resource scheduling. In: Proceedings of the 20th ACM Symposium on Access Control Models and Technologies, pp. 63–74 (2015)

10. Caron, E., Le, A.D., Lefray, A., Toinard, C.: Definition of security metrics for the cloud computing and security-aware virtual machine placement algorithms. In: 2013 International Conference on Cyber-Enabled Distributed Computing and Knowledge Discovery, pp. 125–131. IEEE (2013)

11. Dhanya, D., Arivudainambi, D.: Dolphin partner optimization based secure and qualified virtual machine for resource allocation with streamline security analysis. Peer-to-Peer Netw. Appl. 12(5), 1194–1213 (2019). https://doi.org/10.1007/s12083-019-00765-9

12. Ding, W., et al.: DFA-VMP: an efficient and secure virtual machine placement strategy under cloud environment. Peer-to-Peer Netw. Appl. 11(2), 318–333 (2018). https://doi.org/10.1007/s12083-016-0502-z

13. Garey, M.R., Johnson, D.S.: Computers and Intractability, vol. 174. Freeman, San Francisco (1979)

14. Genssler, P.R., Knodel, O., Spallek, R.G.: Securing virtualized FPGAs for an untrusted cloud. In: Proceedings of the International Conference on Embedded Systems, Cyberphysical Systems, and Applications (ESCS), pp. 3–9. The Steering Committee of The World Congress in Computer Science, Computer Engineering and Applied Computing (2018)

15. Gulmezoglu, B., Eisenbarth, T., Sunar, B.: Cache-based application detection in the cloud using machine learning. In: Proceedings of the 2017 ACM on Asia Conference on Computer and Communications Security, pp. 288–300 (2017)

16. Han, J., Zang, W., Liu, L., Chen, S., Yu, M.: Risk-aware multi-objective optimized virtual machine placement in the cloud. J. Comput. Secur. 26(5), 707–730 (2018)

17. Han, J., Zang, W., Chen, S., Yu, M.: Reducing security risks of clouds through virtual machine placement. In: Livraga, G., Zhu, S. (eds.) DBSec 2017. LNCS, vol. 10359, pp. 275–292. Springer, Cham (2017). https://doi.org/10.1007/978-3-319-61176-1_15

18. Han, Y., Chan, J., Alpcan, T., Leckie, C.: Using virtual machine allocation policies to defend against co-resident attacks in cloud computing. IEEE Trans. Dependable Secure Comput. 14(1), 95–108 (2015)

19. Hu, Y., Wong, J., Iszlai, G., Litoiu, M.: Resource provisioning for cloud computing. In: Proceedings of the 2009 Conference of the Center for Advanced Studies on Collaborative Research, pp. 101–111 (2009)

20. Kiriansky, V., Lebedev, I., Amarasinghe, S., Devadas, S., Emer, J.: DAWG: a defense against cache timing attacks in speculative execution processors. In: 2018 51st Annual IEEE/ACM International Symposium on Microarchitecture (MICRO), pp. 974–987. IEEE (2018)

21. Liang, X., Gui, X., Jian, A., Ren, D.: Mitigating cloud co-resident attacks via groupingbased virtual machine placement strategy. In: 2017 IEEE 36th International Performance Computing and Communications Conference (IPCCC), pp. 1–8. IEEE (2017)

22. Long, V.D., Duong, T.N.B.: Group instance: flexible co-location resistant virtual machine placement in IAAS clouds. In: 2020 IEEE 29th International Conference on Enabling Technologies: Infrastructure for Collaborative Enterprises (WETICE), pp. 64–69. IEEE (2020)

23. Lopez-Pires, F., Baran, B.: Virtual machine placement literature review. arXiv preprint arXiv:1506.01509 (2015)

24. Moon, S.J., Sekar, V., Reiter, M.K.: Nomad: mitigating arbitrary cloud side channels via provider-assisted migration. In: Proceedings of the 22nd ACM SIGSAC Conference on Computer and Communications Security, pp. 1595–1606 (2015)
25. Natu, V., Duong, T.N.B.: Secure virtual machine placement in infrastructure cloud services. In: 2017 IEEE 10th Conference on Service-Oriented Computing and Applications (SOCA), pp. 26–33. IEEE (2017)
26. Ristenpart, T., Tromer, E., Shacham, H., Savage, S.: Hey, you, get off of my cloud: exploring information leakage in third-party compute clouds. In: Proceedings of the 16th ACM Conference on Computer and Communications Security, pp. 199–212 (2009)
27. Sun, Q., Shen, Q., Li, C., Wu, Z.: SeLance: secure load balancing of virtual machines in cloud. In: 2016 IEEE Trustcom/BigDataSE/ISPA, pp. 662–669. IEEE (2016)
28. Varadarajan, V., Zhang, Y., Ristenpart, T., Swift, M.: A placement vulnerability study in multi-tenant public clouds. In: 24th {USENIX} Security Symposium ({USENIX} Security 15), pp. 913–928 (2015)
29. Yu, S., Gui, X., Tian, F., Yang, P., Zhao, J.: A security-awareness virtual machine placement scheme in the cloud. In: 2013 IEEE 10th International Conference on High Performance Computing and Communications and 2013 IEEE International Conference on Embedded and Ubiquitous Computing, pp. 1078–1083. IEEE (2013)
30. Yuchi, X., Shetty, S.: Enabling security-aware virtual machine placement in IAAS clouds. In: 2015 MILCOM IEEE Military Communications Conference, pp. 1554–1559. IEEE (2015)
31. Zhang, T., Zhang, Y., Lee, R.B.: CloudRadar: a real-time side-channel attack detection system in clouds. In: Monrose, F., Dacier, M., Blanc, G., Garcia-Alfaro, J. (eds.) RAID 2016. LNCS, vol. 9854, pp. 118–140. Springer, Cham (2016). https://doi.org/10.1007/978-3-319-45719-2_6
32. Zhang, Y., Li, M., Bai, K., Yu, M., Zang, W.: Incentive compatible moving target defense against VM-colocation attacks in clouds. In: Gritzalis, D., Furnell, S., Theoharidou, M. (eds.) SEC 2012. IAICT, vol. 376, pp. 388–399. Springer, Heidelberg (2012). https://doi.org/10.1007/978-3-642-30436-1_32

Risk Analysis Automation Process in IT Security for Cloud Applications

Daniele Granata(✉)[iD], Massimiliano Rak[iD], and Giovanni Salzillo[iD]

Department of Engineering, University of Campania Luigi Vanvitelli, Aversa, Italy
{daniele.granata,massimiliano.rak,
giovanni.salzillo}@unicampania.it

Abstract. Modern Secure Development Life Cycles recognize that there is a need to (i) perform a risk assessment to identify the threats that a system is facing and (ii) a risk rating procedure to prioritize the development and maintenance activities. However, such processes are hardly applicable in the development of Cloud-based applications, due to the cost (money and time) that such procedures imply. This article aims at addressing such an issue by proposing a technique, compatible with the Security-By-Design development methodologies, that automates the threat modeling and risk evaluation of a system, reducing the costs and requiring the developers with just a limited set of security skills. Through the proposed approach, the software system is analyzed to identify the threats that affect the system assets, ranking the level of risk associated with each threat and suggesting a set of countermeasures in standard terms; the process requires minimal user interaction. The proposed technique was implemented through a dedicated tool and validated against a simple case study.

Keywords: Threat modelling · Risk analysis · Automated analysis · Cloud application · Cybersecurity · Cloud

1 Introduction

The Cloud Computing paradigm relies on a service-based approach and on the delegation of resources and services. Due to the large spread and the pervasiveness of these IT solutions, their security become a hard requirement for the development of Cloud applications: as a matter of fact, the large exposition over the Internet of Cloud applications and the new regulations (e.g. GDPR, NIS Directive, Cybersecurity Act) impose to take into account strict security and privacy requirements.

However, it is not easy to take into account security into application development and the security of Cloud applications is a known issue, especially due to the loss of control over resources and on the code, often managed by third parties. In particular, Cloud-native applications often rely on micro-services architectures and/or on the integration of Commercial-Off-The-Shelf (COTS) components, an approach that has great advantages in terms of costs and time-to-market, but heavily affects the security aspects.

Existing Secure Development Life Cycles (SDLC) relies on the idea of taking into account security from the very early design phases (in a *Security-by-Design* perspective). However, threat modeling, identification of countermeasures, weakness and vulnerability identification, security and penetration testing are time- and cost- expensive

© Springer Nature Switzerland AG 2022
D. Ferguson et al. (Eds.): CLOSER 2021, CCIS 1607, pp. 47–68, 2022.
https://doi.org/10.1007/978-3-031-21637-4_3

procedures, which hardly match with the market needs of fast adaptation to new requirements and the fast release of new functionalities.

We suggest the adoption of a technique that automates, as much as possible, the threat modeling and the risk analysis processes, two activities always considered in existing SDLC, like the Microsoft and CISCO ones, that commonly imply the involvement of (costly) security experts. The proposed approach relies on the experiences and the proposals made in [7, 11] and extends them by taking into account additional factors, simplifying and empowering at the same time the evaluation procedure.

The original contributions, with respect to the state of art, focus on an enhancement of the above-cited model-based risk assessment technique, applying it to Cloud applications, and in particular, we propose:

1. An enhancement of the MACM Cloud application graph-based model;
2. an automated threat identification according to both assets and protocols;
3. an automated threat agent identification;
4. An automated risk ranking process;
5. a tool that implements the approach.

The remainder of the paper is organized as follows: the next Sect. 2 outlines the state of art and the existing solutions for threat and risk assessment automation. Section 3 summarizes the proposed approach and the steps of our methodology, which are described in detail in the following sections. Section 4 is devoted to the description of our graph-based model, Sect. 5 describes how we automatically generate the threat lists and, finally, Sect. 6 is devoted to risk rating. The methodology was applied on a simple, but common case study in Sect. 7. Section 8 summarizes the conclusions and future work.

2   State of the Art

Over the past decade, security has become a critical issue, opening as a consequence several research lines on threat modelling and risk analysis. In this section are outlined some of the most interesting readings in the state of the art.

Xiong et al. [28] presented a systematic literature review of the existing threat modeling approaches. They collected and classified research papers in clusters, based on the threat modeling formalism (graphical or formal), on whether the approach is focused on a specific attack type and application, or the validation (empirical or theoretical). According to state of the art analysis, we invite the interested reader to deepen the existing automated [15, 18–20, 22, 29] and semi-automated [4, 26] threat modeling approaches.

Schaad et al. [25] proposed a STRIDE-based threat modelling technique for software architecture diagrams. They introduced their own conceptual data model, consisting of assets, asset shapes and components. These concepts can be used to describe software systems and perform security evaluations. Additionally, they implemented a supporting tool, TAM^2, that performs an automated threat analysis, based on the described assets.

Casola et al. [10] proposed a Security-by-Design methodology to evaluate the security of IoT systems by the means of an almost automated process for threat modeling and risk assessment. Their approach also helps at identifying the security controls to implement in order to mitigate the existing security risks. .

The OWASP Foundation introduced its risk rating methodology [27], providing a quantitative evaluation of the risks through two indicators: Likelihood and Impact. These indicators are broken down and combined to determine the overall severity of the risk. Among the considered factors there are the threat agents skills, the ease of discovery/exploitation of a vulnerability, or the consequent loss of Confidentiality, Integrity, Availability, or Accountability (CIAA).

Another risk assessment methodology is the CORAS project, which consists of a framework for model-based risk assessment of security-critical systems. This framework consists of eight steps, starting from the system modelling (UML is supported), through the risk estimation and identification, till the risk treatment. Additionally, a tool is available to support on-the-fly modeling using all kinds of CORAS diagrams [2].

Moreover, the Carnegie Mellon University released the *Operationally Critical Threat, Asset, and Vulnerability Evaluation* (OCTAVE) methodology [5], a risk management framework that defines a risk-based strategic assessment and planning technique for assessing the security of a small to medium business organization. The methodology, thought to be led by a small, interdisciplinary team (three to five people), provides the base criteria to perform risk identification, analysis and evaluation.

The state of the art highlights, as can be seen especially from the literature review in [28], that a large part of the existing methodologies to model threats still involves several manual tasks, thus symbolizing that most threat modeling work remains human-driven, time-consuming and error-prone. At the same time, there is the trend to model systems with a higher degree of automation and to automate security analysis. Still, the risk rating methodology landscape is mainly manual, although the quantitative rating automation would certainly improve and speed up the security evaluation of many software products, even during the early design stages. Accordingly, there is a wide need for automating the full process, leaving to humans only the role of final control result and evaluation. This work represents a step forward in this direction.

3 Methodology

According to the NIST SP-800-160 [24], the development of security-critical application relies on a clear Threat Modeling [21], defined as *a systematic process of identifying, analyzing, documenting, and mitigating security threats to a software system.*

The methodology we propose automates as much as possible the threat modeling and risk analysis process, enabling its integration in the security-by-design development methodologies, like the one proposed in [11] and extended in [9]. We produce a list of possible threats and suggest a list of countermeasures in terms of security controls that should be verified before deploying the application in production, after a simplified modeling phase and with minimal user interaction. It is worth noticing that the list of threats is not guaranteed to be complete. A discussion on the completeness and validation is presented in Sect. 5.

A Threat, according to the NIST [24] publication, is *an event or condition that has the potential for causing asset loss and the undesirable consequences or impact from such loss*. Clearly, the identification of all the possible malicious events is a very complex task. Moreover, several threats might be related to design choices, to the involved technologies and/or to custom code development. In order to automate their identification in a generic Cloud application, we model a threat as a triple: $Threat\ Agent,\ Asset,\ Behaviour$.

Based on the available literature [6, 12, 14], we define **Threat Agent** an actor that maliciously acts to generate a threat event against a SuA (System under Attack). An **Asset** is, according to the NIST [24], *an item of value to achievement of organizational mission/business objectives*. We define **Behaviour** the natural language description of a malicious event. It is worth noticing that this description is relevant because it gives to the security expert the information to clearly identify the issues that must be mitigated.

In our methodology, we focus on technical aspects, so we consider only the technological components of the system under attack as possible assets. We have identified different **Asset Types**, that are the classes of assets that are currently supported by our automated process. The list of supported asset types is described in Sect. 4.

Our automation process relies on a catalogue of threats, that collect the possible malicious *Behaviours* for each identified *Asset Type*, enriched by a set of additional information. In particular, for each threat (i) we outline which security requirement in the CIA triad (Confidentiality, Integrity, Availability) is affected and (ii) we classify the threat according to the STRIDE classification [17]. It is worth noticing that the catalogue collects the threat behaviours, while the Threat Model, i.e. the list of specific threats (the above-described triples), will be identified through our algorithms, taking into account the characteristics of the system under analysis.

As illustrated in Fig. 1, our approach relies on three steps, and it requires the user interaction only at the start of the procedure (during system modeling) and at end of the procedure (during the risk rating phase).

The first phase aims at identifying the application architecture and, in particular, the *Assets* involved in the system and their interactions. Section 4 summarizes the main steps involved in this phase, which is the one that needs major user interaction.

The second step, described in Sect. 5, is devoted to Threat Model generation: we identify the possible threats that affect the system, taking into account the asset types and the relationship among them.

The Risk Rating phase, described in Sect. 6, evaluates the probability associated with each threat according to the OWASP methodology, estimating the needed parameters for the evaluation thanks to the information generated by the model and the collected catalogues.

It is worth noticing that the methodology does not assume any user interaction, except during the modelling phase and at end of the process (to evaluate the impact of threats on the business, which can be evaluated only by the system owner).

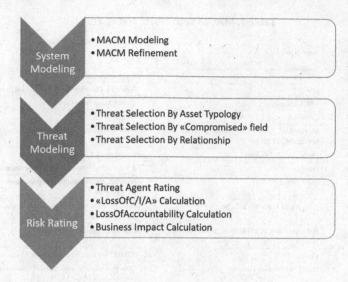

Fig. 1. The steps of the proposed methodology.

4   System Modeling

The system Modeling phase relies on the MACM (Multi-Application Cloud Composition Model) formalism [23], a graph-based model in which each node of the graph represents a component of the system, and each edge characterizes the existing relationship between two different components.

The MACM offers a simple way to synthesize an application architecture, focusing on its main components, thus enabling the automation of the security evaluation for the assessed systems.

In the MACM formalism, a node models an asset and it is characterized by a primary label, that identifies the asset class, and may have a secondary label, which further specifies the primary class. Note that Labels affects the relationship in which a node can be involved. Moreover, each node has a set of properties that better describe more specific attributes. A mandatory property is the *Asset Type*, which specifies the functional behaviour of the asset. The allowed *Asset Types* for a node depends on the labels. The *Labels* and the supported *Asset Types* are listed and described in Table 1.

In this work, we extended the MACM by introducing the concept of *Data*. As shown in Fig. 1, each data is expressed by the *Data* label and represents the data stored, for example, in a database or a configuration file.

Additionally, the relationships between the nodes are modelled as (directed) labelled edges. The edge labels (*relationships* from now on) constraint the allowed labels of source and target nodes. Moreover, the relationships may have properties that specify additional details about the link nature. Table 2 summarizes the currently supported MACM relationships and outlines the allowed labels for the source and target nodes.

An example is the *hosts* relationship among two services, which outlines that a service is offered by another service. To clarify the nature of the hosts relationship, in Fig. 2 are shown three different *host* scenarios for a given service (a MySQL server). In

Table 1. MACM node labels and assets.

Primary label	Secondary label	Asset type(s)	Description
CSC		CSC.Human	A customer that uses services
CSP		CSP	A Service Provider like Amazon, Google, or a ISP
Service	IaaS	VM, Container	Virtual Machine or Containers
Service	PaaS	Container	Containers
Service	SaaS	Service.Web, Service.DB, Service.IOTGW, Service.MQTTBroker	Software (typically COTS) offered as a service
service	CaaS	Docker LXC Container	Container as a Service
Network	WAN	Internet	A wide area Network, typically the Internet
Network	LAN	WiFi, Wired	Network, the assets differs depending on the involved technologies
Network	PAN	Network.BLE, Network.ZigBee	Personal Area Network, the assets differs depending on the involved technologies
HW		HW.server, HW.PC, HW.micro, HW.IOTDevice, HW.UE	A physical hosting hardware
ECN		Device.MEC	A MEC Server acting as an Edge Compute Node
Data		Data.Configuration Data.DB	Data processed by a service (i.e. database tables, configuration files ...)

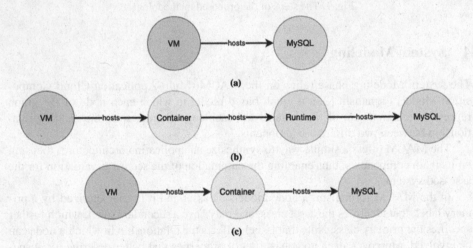

Fig. 2. Layered service virtualization.

Fig. 2a, a Virtual Machine hosts a standalone MySQL service. In this case, the software is installed directly on the VM operating system (as in a typical IaaS scenario). On the other hand, Fig. 2b depicts a more complex architecture, whereas the MySQL service is installed on-top of a run-time environment (i.e. a base Linux image) executed by a container engine (in a CaaS perspective), and hosted, in turn, by a virtual machine. This is the case in which a developer extends a base image, for example, a docker image, by adding its own software components (typically a custom software layer). In the last picture, Fig. 2c, the software component is hosted directly on top of the containerization engine, i.e. the MySQL docker image pulled and run as-is from the docker-hub. Note that, even in this case the image still contains the run-time environment as in Fig. 2b, though it's hidden to the modeller. This consideration makes Fig. 2b and 2c similar from an architectural point of view, but very different from a security analysis perspective. Finally, note the use of different colours to specify different components in the layered view.

In order to describe the way in which VMs or services uses data, we extended the relationship types introducing the *processes* relationship. It indicates that any service (IaaS, PaaS or SaaS), or an ECN [13] is directly responsible for accessing the data. For example, a Virtual Machine (i.e. a IaaS service) can process the configuration files provided by the user to set up the environment.

Table 2. Relationship in MACM models.

Relationship	Source node(s)	Target node(s)
Uses	CSC, service (IaaS, SaaS, PaaS), IOTDevice, IoTGW	service (IaaS, SaaS, PaaS), IOTDevice, IoTGW
Provides	CSP	service (IaaS, SaaS, PaaS), Network
Hosts	Service (IaaS, PaaS), HW	service (IaaS, SaaS, PaaS)
Connects	Network	HW, CSP, CSC
Processes	Service (IaaS, SaaS, PaaS), ECN	Data

After modeling the system, the MACM is then enriched during a refinement phase. In this phase, the modeler provides for each service the *audit* property. This attribute indicates the operation logging level on the service and can have three different values:

- Fully Traceable, i.e. all accesses and actions to the service are stored automatically.
- Approximate Logs or Possibly Traceable, i.e. not all logs are automatically collected or they can be collected manually.
- No tracks.

This information is provided by the system expert in order to collect all information needed to assess the system security.

5 Threat Modelling

The enriched system information available through the MACM, are used to identify the threats affecting each component of the system, building the Threat Model, that acts as a basis to perform security evaluations.
Previous works [8, 9, 11] relies on a Threat Catalogue, built in the context of the MUSA H2020 project, that organizes the threats according to their asset type. The threats of the catalogue were collected using a set of well -nown sources, like the OWASP top threats and referenced scientific paper, maintaining the link to the adopted source in the catalogue. In this work, we focused on introducing a new threat catalogue, available as open-data[1]. The catalogue describes the threats with 8 parameters, as shown in Table 3.

---

[1] In case you are interested, please send an email to the authors to request the latest version of the catalogue.

Table 3. Threat catalogue template.

Threat catalogue field	Description
Threat	A synthetic high-level label of the behaviour
Asset type	The asset typology to which the threat is subject
Relationship	Relation type
Protocol	Protocol used in the communication that produces the threat
Role in relationship	Role in communication
Behaviour	Detailed description of the threat
PreCondition	How much confidentiality, integrity and availability have to be compromised in order to perform the threat
PostCondition	How much the threat compromises the confidentiality, integrity and availability
STRIDE	Stride classification [1]
Compromised	Which assets the malicious behaviour compromises

A threat can be linked to an asset (asset type) or a communication protocol. For this reason, some fields may be left blank. For example, if a threat affects a specific asset typology, i.e. the *Read DB Configuration* threat for a *service. DB* asset type, both the relationship and role fields are left unspecified. The *PreCondition* and the *PostCondition* fields, instead, are provided in the [ValueC,ValueI,ValueA] format. In particular, the first value indicates the compromising level of confidentiality, the second one refers to integrity and the last one to availability. The possible values are:

- n (none), requirement not compromised
- p (partial), requirement partially compromised
- f (full), requirement totally compromised

As an example, the *Update Injection* threat has [p,n,n] as *PreCondition* and [p,p,n] as *PostCondition* values. This means that the confidentiality must be partially compromised in order to implement this threat and that, as a consequence, the attacker would compromise the integrity of the assets by exploiting this threat.

Additionally, the *Compromised* field indicates the asset which is compromised by the malicious behaviour and it can assume the following values:

- *self*, if the threat compromises only the node specified by the asset type;
- *source(relation)*, when it compromises the node pointing from the arch;
- *target(relation)*, when it compromises the node pointed by the arch;

It is worth to note that when the *Compromised* field is source or target, the argument *relation* can be *uses,connects* or *hosts*.

Our threat modeling technique provides an algorithm to select the threats that compromise the software components and another algorithm used to select the threats that compromise the data. The first one is described in pseudo-code 1.

Algorithm 1. ThreatModelGeneration(MACM).

Require: MACM
Ensure: Threat Model
1: **for** $asset$ in $MACM.nodes$ **do**
2:      $behaviours \leftarrow getBehavioursFromCatalogue(asset.type)$
3:      **for** $behaviour$ in $behaviours$ **do**
4:          $threat \leftarrow (asset, behaviour)$
5:          $ThreatModel.add(threat)$
6:      **end for**
7:      $Neighborbehaviours \leftarrow getNeighborbehaviours(asset, asset.relationships)$
8:      **for** $Neighborbehaviour$ in $Neighborbehaviours$ **do**
9:          $UndirectedThreat \leftarrow (asset, Neighborbehaviour)$
10:         $ThreatModel.add(UndirectedThreat)$
11:     **end for**
12:     $ProtocolBehaviours \leftarrow getProtocolBehaviours(asset.relationships)$
13:     **for** $ProtocolBehaviour$ in $ProtocolBehaviours$ **do**
14:         $ProtocolThreat \leftarrow (asset, ProtocolBehaviour)$
15:         $ThreatModel.add(ProtocolThreat)$
16:     **end for**
17: **end for**

The algorithm requires a MACM as input and returns all the threats the components are subjected to, by constructing the threat model in three consecutive steps. In the first step, for each component (i.e. the asset), the *getBehavioursFromCatalogue* function selects the malicious behaviours collected in the new threat catalogue, indexed by AssetType.

Each asset is also subject to the threats caused by the communication with other components, Accordingly, in the second step, through the *getNeighborbehaviours* function, the algorithm selects all the threats that indirectly compromise the asset due to the nearby component. In particular, the function considers all the neighboured nodes of the asset and selects all the malicious behaviour that compromised the asset (considering the Compromised field). For example, if an asset A_1 uses the asset A_2 and, considering T_1 as the threat A_1 is subjected to, if *Compromised* field of T_1 is *target(uses)*, therefore T_1 affects also A_2.

The last step of the algorithm considers all the protocols specified by each *uses* relationship of the asset. The *getProtocolBehaviours* function selects the threats each protocol is subjected to and inserts them into the threat model.

Differently from the threat definition introduced in [16] and reported in Sect. 3, in this extension, we define a threat with the couple $Asset, Behaviour$, as the *threat agent* is defined further in Sect. 6 for the risk calculation.

Another asset to carefully evaluate is the Data asset. For this asset, our catalogue considers only three threats: loss of Confidentiality (C), loss of Integrity(I) and loss of Availability(A). We consider three *level* of threats: none (there is no loss of C/I/A), partial (the data are partially compromised in terms of C/I/A) and full (data are no more reliable in terms of C/I/A).

The level of Loss of Confidentiality is calculated as follows: if there is at least one node that processes the data, then loss of confidentiality is the maximum value between the *PostCondition* field of all the threats affecting the asset that process the data. If this value is n, then, our technique verifies if there exists any path from any service towards the data through the *uses* relations. If any node in the path has at least one threat that partially compromises the confidentiality, then the Loss Of Confidentiality of the data is partial. Similarly, the technique calculates the loss of integrity.

Instead, the level of loss of availability for the data asset is set to the minimum value. This is due to the fact that the unavailability of the service does not necessarily compromise the availability of the data as the data may also be available thanks to other services.

6   Risk Rating

The Threat Modeling clearly identifies the threats menacing the system under analysis, however addressing them all could not be compatible with time-to-market and application costs. The Risk Analysis aims at offering a (rough) evaluation of the risk (i.e. the probability that a threat would occur) in order to prioritize the implementation of the security controls.

We adopted the Risk Rating Methodology proposed by OWASP [27], which evaluate the risk through the composition of two indicators: *Likelihood* and *Impact*. *Likelihood* is an indicator that expresses how likely a threat agent would implement a threat. OWASP gives a quantitative evaluation, by considering two sets of factors: Threat Agent Factors and Vulnerability Factors. The first ones are related to the group of threat agents, considering: *skill Level*, *motive*, *opportunity* and *size*. On the other hand, the *vulnerability factors* are related to the vulnerabilities needed to exploit a specific threat and take into account the *ease of discovery*, *ease of exploit* , *awareness* and *intrusion detection*.

Even the *Impact* relies on two set of factors, namely the *technical* and the *business* factors. The technical impact is estimated taking into account how a threat affects the security requirement of the asset in terms of the *Loss of Confidentiality*, *Loss of Integrity*, *Loss of Availability* and *Loss of Accountability*.

Last but not least, the *business factors* take into account what is important to the company running the application, evaluating the *financial damage*, *reputation damage*, *non-compliance* and *privacy violation*.

The OWASP methodology offers a descriptive criteria to assign to each of the above factors a number between 1 and 10. Likelihood and Impact will assume a level of risk (*Low*, *Medium* or *High*) if the average of the values of their factors is respectively in the range 1–3, 4–6 or 7–10. The risk value of a threat is assigned through a table that assigns the final risk level according to the Likelihood and Impact levels.

Thanks to our approach, the Threat Agents and the behaviour of the threats can be determined in advance, so it is possible to evaluate 12 out of 16 factors without any user involvement. The only factors for which we suggest a default value are related to business impact, which is strictly related to the context of the execution of the application and its market considerations.

6.1   Threat Agent Selection and Rating

As already outlined, Threat Agents are *any person or thing that has the power to act to cause, carry, transmit, or support a threat.* In a security assessment process, the identification of Threat Agents is a fundamental part and its results influence the Risk Rating activities. In this phase, we built a technique to select the threat agents the system can be attacked and use them to calculate the OWASP threat agent risk parameters. In order to identify possible threat agents, we adopted the taxonomy proposed in [6].

The threat agent classification associates to each class of threat agents a set of attributes and proposes a mapping that outlines which are the attribute values associated with each Threat Agent. Table 4 summarizes the attributes and the possible values of the attribute.

In order to select the Threat Agents (TAs) and evaluate the risk associate to each of them, we classify the proposed attributes in two classes: (i) attributes useful to identify the TAs that are meaningful for the system under analysis and (ii) attributes useful to risk evaluation.

In the selection process we concentrate on the first class, which, according to our consideration are *Intent, Access, Outcome, Objective.* Accordingly we identified four questions to which the system owner should answer, that enable us to select the TAs.

– Q1: Are there someone who can gain an advantage by implementing a cyber threat against your system?
– Q2: Do you trust all employees and do you assume that they are not a possible Threat agent?
– Q3: What are the goals of the attackers that represent the most threat to you?
– Q4: What could be the expected results of a possible attacker in the phases of a possible attack on the software system?

Q1 identifies the threat agent's hostility. Q2 is used to consider the threat agents that have internal access to the application. For example, if the user marks the employees (or partners who have access to confidential data) as "trusted", these categories are removed from the final threat agent list. Q3 and Q4, instead, allow multiple answers and apply the filter to the threat agents in relation to the steps they take to attack the system and the desired result of the attacker. The answers to these questions are used to select the threat agent categories. For example, Terrorist or Data miner can not be selected if the user considers "Embarrassment" the only outcome. The result of the first step is a threat agent list containing a description of the threat agent and common actions he takes to attack the target.

Table 4. Threat agent attributes [16].

Attribute	Description	Attribute values
Access	Privileged position of the target infrastructure	Internal, External
Intent	Whether the agent intends harm	Hostile, Not Hostile
Limits	Legal and ethical limits of threat agent	Code of Conduct, Legal, Extra-legal Minor, Extra-legal Major
Outcome	Primary goal of threat agent	Acquisition, Business Advantage, Damage, Embarrassment, Technical Advantage
Objective	Method agent uses for achieving goals	Copy, Deny, Destroy, Damage, Take, All
Resources	Available time, money and technological means	Individual, Club, Contest, Team, Organization, Government
Skills	Special training and expertise	None, Minimal, Operational, Adept
Visibility	How hidden are identity and actions	Overt, Covert, Clandestine, Don't Care

Table 5. Mapping OWASP Threat Agent parameters with TAL parameters.

OWASP parameter	TAL parameter
Skill level	Skill
Motive	Limits, Outcome, Intent
Opportunity	Access, Resources, Visibility
Size	Resources

The evaluation of the OWASP parameters relating to threat agents is based on the categories resulting from the questionnaire. Each category has a threat agent library (TAL [6]) attribute set that describes it. Each attribute has a score which we use to calculate the OWASP values, considering the mapping shown in Table 5. For example, we assume that OWASP Motive depends only on *Intent*, *Outcome* and *Limits* and it is calculated as follows:

$$OWASPMotive = \frac{\frac{Intent}{2} + \frac{Outcome}{5} + \frac{Limits}{4}}{3}x10 \qquad (1)$$

For multiple responses related to attributes (such as Outcome values), the considered value is the average of the single associated ones.

The process in this way calculates four OWASP parameters for each category. In order to produce the parameters relating to the system, it is necessary to evaluate the combination of all the OWASP parameters for each category of the Threat Agent Selection result. For example, the total OWASP Motive value is given by the formula:

$$OWASPMotiveTOT = \frac{\sum_{i=1}^{N} A_i M_i}{A_{tot}} \tag{2}$$

N represents the number of categories resulting from the Wizard and M_i the OWASP score of the reason relating to the i-th category and d A_i instead represents the i-th weight assigned by the user to the single output category through a Low-Medium-High qualitative approach. In this way, the user decides which output category is more dangerous for the overall application.

6.2 Vulnerability Factors

To evaluate the risk of a threat, we still miss the factors related to the vulnerabilities. According to OWASP, a security expert, should make such evaluations, taking into account (i) how to implement an attack, exploiting the vulnerabilities to implement the threat, and (ii) which are the effect of the threat over the asset. However, as outlined in Sect. 5, we collected in the catalogue the full set of possible threats in terms of $< Asset, Behaviour >$ together with additional information, namely the affected security requirements and the STRIDE classification of the threat.

This enabled us to make an evaluation of the threats and to identify the default value for eight of the associated factors. In practice, we evaluated in advance all the possible threats assigning the values to avoid any additional requests. In future works we aim at improving such an evaluation, through additional attributes to the MACM model: knowing the technologies that implement a node, as an example, it would be possible to make a search over threat intelligence knowledge bases, like NVD[2] or the assigned MITRE CVE, CWE, ATT&CK or CAPEC, and perform additional automated evaluations.

6.3 Impact Factors

In OWASP, the *Impact* relies on two set of factors, namely the *technical* and the *business* factors.

The *Business factors* takes into account what is important to the company running the application, considering the *Financial damage*, *Reputation damage*, *Non-compliance* and *Privacy violation*. These parameters are pre-calculated with a default value and can be changed later on by the user. Each threat was associated with one or more STRIDE categories [17], i.e. Spoofing, Tampering, Repudiation, Information Disclosure, Denial of Services and Elevation of Privileges. Then we ask the user to express the impact factor of each STRIDE category over the overall system (it is possible to make a per-asset request if the user is interested to a finer grain evaluation). Finally, we evaluate the impact of a threat on an asset considering the higher impact among the ones that the user declared for each STRIDE category to which the threat belongs to.

The most critical part, is the estimation of the technical impact that takes into account how a threat affects the security requirements of the asset in terms of the *Loss*

---

[2] National Vulnerability Database NVD, https://nvd.nist.gov.

of Confidentiality, the *Loss of Integrity*, the *Loss of Availability* and the *Loss of Accountability*.

In order to calculate the Loss of Confidentiality, Integrity, Availability, we use the *PostCondition* field of each threat the asset is subjected to. By considering the Confidentiality, for example, in the *PostCondition* field, the OWASP Loss of Confidentiality (LoC) value is taken from the Table 6.

Table 6. Mapping between PostCondition Confidentiality and OWASP LossOfConfidentiality.

PostCondition Confidentiality value	OWASP LoC
n	1
p	4
f	9

Similarly, the LossofIntegrity (LoI) and LossofAvailability (LoA) parameters are obtained by considering the respective values from the *PostCondition* field.

It should be noted that for the *Data* assets, the values of *LoC*, *LoI* and *LoA* are obtained by considering the values of loss of confidentiality, integrity and availability, as shown in Sect. 5.

The Loss of Accountability factor, instead, depends on how much the threat agent action can be traced. To calculate this factor, we evaluate the *audit* property of the asset (as described in Sect. 4). If the audit property is *fully traceable*, then all the threats have *LoA* equal to 1, because all actions can be traced. If instead the audit property is approximate logs, then *LoA* is set to 4.

Finally, if the asset has no logs, all the threats applied to the asset have a Loss of Accountability equal to 9.

6.4   Overall Evaluation and Input Collection

As a summary, for each threat, we are automatically able to estimate 12 over 16 of the factors requested by the OWASP methodology. However, the number of possible threats remains pretty long and involving the user in order to collect the last four factors for each of the (tens, if not hundreds) identified possible threats is unpractical. Accordingly, we followed a simplified approach: each threat was associated with one or more STRIDE [17] categories, Spoofing, Tampering, Reputation, Information Disclosure, Denial of Services and Elevation of Privileges. Then we ask the user to express the impact factor of each STRIDE category over the overall system (it is possible to make a per-asset request if the user is interested in a finer grain evaluation). Finally, we evaluate the impact of a threat on an asset considering the higher impact among the ones that the user declared for each STRIDE category to which the threat belongs to.

The final likelihood value is obtained by averaging the Threat Agent and Vulnerability parameters. Similarly, the final impact value is calculated by averaging the Business and Technical factors.

As a final result, we are able to make a detailed risk analysis, outlining, for each threat, the associated Risk Level (as a value Low, Medium or High).

The validation of the proposed evaluation is, however, almost impossible, as often happens in Risk analysis approaches. We rely on a well-established methodology (suggested by OWASP) that assigns a relevant role to the security experts. Our technique anticipates the work of the security experts so that it is possible to automate the process, delegating it to the developers, even with limited security skills. As a consequence, it is possible to involve the (costly) experts only for the result validation or in specific phases of the project development.

7   Case Study

To validate the proposed technique, we describe in this section a very common application, typically executed on a Cloud infrastructure: an e-commerce site developed on top of Wordpress. Wordress (WP) is an open source content management system, which allows the creation and distribution of a website with textual and multimedia contents, which can be managed and updated dynamically. In our case study, the WP web application is hosted on a Cloud virtual machine, on top of an Apache web server and it is interfaced with a MySQL database that stores and processes the data it manages. To enable scalability, the WordPress component can be deployed multiple times, reusing the single database instance (that can scale only vertically, i.e. adding memory and/or CPU to the hosting VM). A Load Balancer (LB) distributes the client requests to the connected WP instances. The developer simply customizes the WP instances, e.g. through custom themes and plugins.

Even if the development of such systems is simple and commonly relies on very limited skills of the developer/system administrators, the application might manage money and personal data, so it has strict security requirements. It should be noted that an incredible amount of Wordpress instances on the web are vulnerable (see [3]), due to incorrect security planning and management.

7.1   Modeling

As previously described, the first step of the proposed methodology provides the formal modelling of the system under analysis. In Table 7 are reported the nodes of our case-study Wordpress application, whereas Fig. 3 shows the complete MACM model for the application.

Generally speaking, the *IaaS* nodes can be of *VM* or *container* asset type, while *SaaS* can be of *Web Application*, *Database*. New asset types can be easily added, as an example the MACM model was extended to support IoT systems in [7]. The (directed) edges of the graph represent the relationship among the nodes. The model adopts few different kind of relationship, namely: *provides*, *hosts*,*uses* and *processes*. The relationship outlines the way in which the different types of components may interact, as an example, the *uses* relationship among two services, outlines that a service uses the capabilities offered by the other. The model allows to associate properties to relationships, e.g. it is possible to specify a *protocol* attribute to a *uses* relationship, whose value indicates the protocols involved in the interaction.

Table 7. Assets and their types in the case study.

Node	Label	Asset type
Client	CSC	CSC
CSP	CSP	CSP
LB (Load balancer)	SaaS	WebApplication
WP (WordPress)	SaaS	WebApplication
DB (Database)	SaaS	Database
VM (Virtual machine)	IaaS	VirtualMachine

Table 8. Relation between components in case study.

Start node	Relation	End node	Protocol
Client	Uses	LB	https
LB	Uses	Wordpress	https
Wordpress	Uses	Database	mysql
Database	Processes	Database data	–
VMs	Processes	Configuration data	–
VM	Hosts	Wordpress	–
VM	Hosts	LB	–
VM	Hosts	DB	–
CSP	Provides	VMs	–

Each label affects the colour of the nodes, while attributes are not visible in the picture. As anticipated, the system is composed of a Cloud Service Provider (e.g. Amazon or a private Cloud) that *provides* three virtual machines. which are labeled as *IaaS*, and their Asset Type is *VM*, e.g. virtual machine. One VM *hosts* a Load Balancer service while the other two VMs *hosts* respectively a WordPress instance and a MySQL database instance. We modeled the Load Balancer (LB) and WordPress (WP) as *SaaS* nodes and we set their Asset Type as *Web Application*. The MySQL instance, instead, was labeled as a *SaaS*, but with *Database* (DB) value as Asset Type. The LB *uses* the WP that, in turn, uses the DB. The Customer(s) (modeled as a *CSC* node) uses the LB node, that acts as application interface. Tables 7 and 8 summarize the model.

7.2 Threat Selection

According to our case study, the assets are the ones already anticipated in the previous sections and summarized in Tables 1 and 2 of the Modeling section. Applying the proposed approach we produce a list of threats that we have summarized, for simplicity' sake we summarized some of the threats per asset in Table 9. A list of Threats is not compatible with the length of the paper. Analyzing the tables it is possible to outline, as an example, that Wordpress can be exposed to threats such as Injection. Other

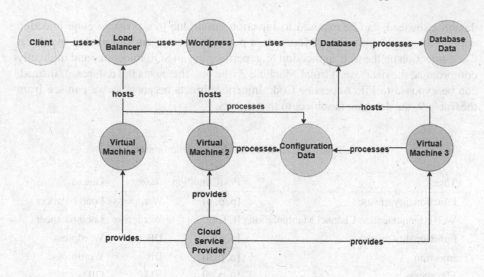

Fig. 3. MACM Wordpress Case study.

threats that affect the VMs are linked to data and policy violation such as Data Breaches and Authorization abuse. Moreover, data can be breached by threat agents in the SQL database, partially compromising the confidentiality of the data.

Table 9. Threat selection results per asset (snippet).

Threat	PostCondition	Asset
Injection	[n, p, n]	Wordpress
Sensitive data exposure	[p, n, n]	Wordpress
System manipulation	[f, f, f]	Wordpress
Read injection	[p, n, n]	DB
File access	[p, p, p]	DB
Code injection	[n, f, n]	DB
Data breach	[p, n, n]	VM
Crash	[n, p, f]	VM
Authorization abuse	[p, p, n]	VM
...	...	...

As described in Algorithm 1 some other threats are caused by the communication with other services considering the threat Compromised field. Some results are collected in Table 10 that outlines the threats compromising the Asset that are due to a specific component. For example, Wordpress can be exposed to Functionality Misuse caused by the communication with Load Balancer (that is affected by that threat). Mysql database, instead, can be exposed to Injection threat due to a possible code injection applied on a web application. Moreover, a possible threat agent can exploit the threat Code Injection on the web application (e.g. performing an SQL injection) and indirectly compromise the database. Virtual Machine 3 (the one that hosts the database), instead, can be exposed to File Access or Code Injection threats because, as we can see from the Table 9, the database is subject to that threats.

Table 10. Threat selection results due to compromised field.

Threat	PostCondition	Asset	Due to
Functionality misuse	[p, p, p]	Wordpress	Load balancer
Web communication Channel Manipulation	[f, f, f]	Wordpress	Load balancer
Functionality misuse	[p, p, p]	DB	Wordpress
Injection	[n, p, n]	DB	Wordpress
File access	[p, p, p]	VM1	DB
Code injection	[n, f, n]	VM1	DB
...	...	...	...

The third part of the algorithm collects the threats related to the protocols used in communications. For the sake of brevity, we have reported those due to the use of the HTTPS protocol in the communication between the Load Balancer and Wordpress in the Table 11.

Table 11. Threats due to HTTPS in LB-Wordpress relation.

Threat	PostCondition	Asset
Eavesdropping	[f, n, n]	WP
Message reply	[n, p, p]	LB
Message injection	[n, p, p]	WP
Message deleting	[n, p, p]	LB
Spoofing users	[n, p, n]	WP
Gaining unauthorized entry to a server or account	[p, p, n]	WP
Denial of services	[n, n, p]	WP
Message modification	[n, p, p]	WP
Message modification	[n, p, p]	LB
...	...	...

A threat agent, for instance, can retrieve data accessing HTTPS communication among Load Balancer and Wordpress or can send some message with a spoofed identity.

As for the data, all the threats of the components that process them are evaluated and loss of confidentiality, integrity and availability are obtained as described in Sect. 5. For *Database Data*, for example, the loss of confidentiality is partial as the threats associated with MySQL compromise at most partially the confidentiality. The integrity of the data is fully compromised because of the *Code Injection* threat that can lead to the complete manipulation of the data. Loss of Availability of the data is, instead, considered as the minimum value.

7.3 Risk Analysis

In order to calculate the risks associated with threats, we firstly apply the Threat Agent Selection and Rating algorithms, described in [16].

In our case study, we assume that the system's cyber-security officer considers only the hostile threat agents. This may be due to the exposure of threats that can bring financial advantage to the agent, especially on Wordpress sites such as e-commerce. We also assumed that the director has the complete trust in the employees, which excludes them from the results. Having made these answers to the questionnaire, the categories interested in attacking the system are described by the Table 12.

Table 12. Results of threat agent selection phase in the example scenario [16].

Category	Description	Common actions
Competitor	Business adversary who competes for resources	Theft of IP or business data
Cyber vandal	Derives thrills from intrusion or destruction of property, without strong agenda	Network/Computing disruption, web hijacking, malware
Irrational individual	Someone with illogical purpose and irrational behavior	Personal violence resulting in physical business disruption
Data miner	Professional data gatherer external to the company	Theft of Personally Identifiable Information, IP or business data
Sensationalist	Attention-grabber who may employ any method for notoriety of fame	Public announcements for PR crises, theft of business data

Let's consider, for example, the OWASP factor Motive for the *Data Miner* agent, as shown in formula (1):

$$DataMinerMotive = \frac{\frac{2}{2} + \frac{3}{5} + \frac{3}{4}}{3}x10 = 7 \tag{3}$$

Accordingly, the OWASP Motive values calculated by (3) give the value 7, which means that threat agents might be strongly motivated to attack the system. A similar approach is used for the OWASP Size, Motive and Opportunity parameters. As already stated, Vulnerability factors are, instead, taken from the threat catalogue. For example, considering the *Code Execution* threat, we produce the Table 14 containing all 8 likelihood scores[3]. As shown in the table, we assumed that all vulnerability parameters are medium (Table 13).

Table 13. Likelihood scores related to injection threat.

Threat agent	Score	Vulnerability	Score
Skill Level	8	Ease of discovery	5
Motive	7	Ease of exploit	5
Opportunity	5	Awareness	5
Size	6	Intrusion detection	5

Impact parameters for *Code Injection* threat are shown in Table 14. As it has [n,f,n] *PostCondition* field, *LossOfC/I/A* parameters are obtained as already shown in the Table 6. This means that an attacker could perform the Code injection completely denying the integrity of the service. Loss of Accountability is instead 4 because considering each asset, the *audit* parameter is on average partial.

In order to obtain the business impact parameters, we used the Stride classification given by the threat catalogue. For example, the Code injection threat is inserted in the stride *Tampering* class, therefore we used the default values for *Tampering* threats. For this reason, we assumed that the threats that involve manipulating the data can lead to high financial damage.

Table 14. Impact scores related to injection threat.

Technical factor	Score	Business impact	Score
Loss of confidentiality	1	Financial damage	7
Loss of integrity	9	Reputation damage	3
Loss of availability	1	Non compliance	3
Loss of accountability	4	Privacy violation	5

At this phase, we are able to calculate the likelihood and impact for each threat. For example, the likelihood for *Code Execution* threat is HIGH, while the impact is MEDIUM.

8 Conclusion

In this paper, we presented a technique that aims at automating threat modelling and risk analysis processes. Using the proposed technique, non-security experts can automate

---

[3] Full report is available on request.

most of the common tasks performed by security professionals, which is considered to be easily integrated with security-by-design development methodologies. It's worth noting that our goal is not to replace the security experts, but to allow them to participate only when absolutely necessary, such as to evaluate and improve the policies, and to verify the correctness of automated choices made during the development.

The proposed approach requires a very simple model of the application and the user to answer to a few questions to perform the risk analysis. We applied the technique to a simple, but common case study. To the best of the researchers' knowledge, no other technique is able to support threat agent identification, threat modeling, and risk analysis without any user interaction except for a few questions in the first step of the methodology.

In future work, we intend to investigate a technique for validating risk analysis processes, including threat intelligence data sets, in order to offer further grants on our results and increase the quality of our risk level assessments.

Furthermore, we want to automate as much as possible the enrichment step of the threat catalogue by collecting data from open data sets and refining risk factor evaluation through specific analysis and testing techniques.

References

1. Microsoft Corporation, The STRIDE Threat Model (2016). https://docs.microsoft.com/en-us/previous-versions/commerce-server/ee823878(v=cs.20)
2. CORAS risk analysis methodology. https://coras.sourceforge.net
3. Abela, R.: Statistics show why wordpress is a popular hacker target (2020). https://www.wpwhitesecurity.com/statistics-70-percent-wordpress-installations-vulnerable/
4. Arsac, W., Bella, G., Chantry, X., Compagna, L.: Multi-attacker protocol validation. J. Autom. Reasoning **46**(3–4), 353–388 (2011)
5. Caralli, R., Stevens, J., Young, L., Wilson, W.: Introducing octave allegro: improving the information security risk assessment process. Technical report CMU/SEI-2007-TR-012, Software Engineering Institute, Carnegie Mellon University, Pittsburgh, PA (2007). https://resources.sei.cmu.edu/library/asset-view.cfm?AssetID=8419
6. Casey, T.: Threat agent library helps identify information security risks, p. 12 (2007). https://doi.org/10.13140/RG.2.2.30094.46406
7. Casola, V.: Toward the automation of threat modeling and risk assessment in IoT systems. Internet of Things, 13 (2019)
8. Casola, V., De Benedictis, A., Rak, M., Rios, E.: Security-by-design in clouds: a security-SLA driven methodology to build secure cloud applications. Procedia Comput. Sci. **97**, 53–62 (2016)
9. Casola, V., De Benedictis, A., Rak, M., Salzillo, G.: A cloud SecDevOps methodology: from design to testing. In: Shepperd, M., Brito e Abreu, F., Rodrigues da Silva, A., Pérez-Castillo, R. (eds.) QUATIC 2020. CCIS, vol. 1266, pp. 317–331. Springer, Cham (2020). https://doi.org/10.1007/978-3-030-58793-2_26
10. Casola, V., De Benedictis, A., Rak, M., Villano, U.: Toward the automation of threat modeling and risk assessment in IoT systems. Internet Things **7**, 100056 (2019)
11. Casola, V., De Benedictis, A., Rak, M., Villano, U.: A novel security-by-design methodology: modeling and assessing security by SLAs with a quantitative approach. J. Syst. Softw. **163**, 110537 (2020)

12. Dobrovoljc, A., Trček, D., Likar, B.: Predicting exploitations of information systems vulnerabilities through attackers' characteristics. IEEE Access **5**, 13 (2017)

13. Ficco, M., Granata, D., Rak, M., Salzillo, G.: Threat modeling of edge-based IoT applications. In: Paiva, A.C.R., Cavalli, A.R., Ventura Martins, P., Pérez-Castillo, R. (eds.) QUATIC 2021. CCIS, vol. 1439, pp. 282–296. Springer, Cham (2021). https://doi.org/10.1007/978-3-030-85347-1_21

14. Fraunholz, D., Anton, S.D., Schotten, H.D.: Introducing GAMfIS: a generic attacker model for information security, p. 6 (2017)

15. Frydman, M., Ruiz, G., Heymann, E., César, E., Miller, B.P.: Automating risk analysis of software design models. Sci. World J. 2014 (2014)

16. Granata, D., Rak., M.: Design and development of a technique for the automation of the risk analysis process in it security. In: Proceedings of the 11th International Conference on Cloud Computing and Services Science - CLOSER, pp. 87–98. INSTICC, SciTePress (2021). https://doi.org/10.5220/0010455200870098

17. Kohnfelder, L., Garg, P.: The threats to our products. Microsoft Interface, Microsoft Corporation, 33 (1999)

18. Kornecki, A.J., Janusz, Z.: Threat modeling for aviation computer security. Crosstalk, 21 (2015)

19. Lenzini, G., Mauw, S., Ouchani, S.: Security analysis of socio-technical physical systems. Comput. Electr. Eng. **47**, 258–274 (2015)

20. Marback, A., Do, H., He, K., Kondamarri, S., Xu, D.: A threat model-based approach to security testing. Softw.: Pract. Experience **43**(2), 241–258 (2013)

21. Marback, A., Do, H., He, K., Kondamarri, S., Xu, D.: A threat model-based approach to security testing. Softw.: Practice and Experience, **43**, 241–258 (2013). https://doi.org/10.1002/spe.2111

22. MUSMAN, S., Turner, A.J.: A game oriented approach to minimizing cybersecurity risk. Saf. Secur. Stud. 27 (2018)

23. Rak, M.: Security assurance of (multi-)cloud application with security SLA composition. In: Au, M.H.A., Castiglione, A., Choo, K.K.R., Palmieri, F., Li, K.C. (eds.) Green, Pervasive, and Cloud Computing. LNCS, vol. 10232, pp. 786–799. Springer, Cham (2017)

24. Ross, R., McEvilley, M., Oren, J.C.: Systems security engineering considerations for a multidisciplinary approach in the engineering of trustworthy secure systems (2016). https://doi.org/10.6028/NIST.SP.800-160v1

25. Schaad, A., Borozdin, M.: Tam: automated threat analysis. In: Proceedings of the 27th Annual ACM Symposium on Applied Computing, pp. 1103–1108. SAC 2012, Association for Computing Machinery, New York, NY, USA (2012). https://doi.org/10.1145/2245276.2231950

26. Singh, S., Tu, H., Allanach, J., Areta, J., Willett, P., Pattipati, K.: Modeling threats. IEEE Potentials **23**(3), 18–21 (2004)

27. Williams, J.: OWASP risk rating methodology (2020). https://owasp.org/www-community/OWASP_Risk_Rating_Methodology

28. Xiong, W., Lagerström, R.: Threat modeling - a systematic literature review. Comput. Secur. **84**, 53–69 (2019)

29. Xu, D., Tu, M., Sanford, M., Thomas, L., Woodraska, D., Xu, W.: Automated security test generation with formal threat models. IEEE Trans. Dependable Secure Comput. **9**(4), 526–540 (2012)

AI Quality Engineering for Machine Learning Based IoT Data Processing

Shelernaz Azimi and Claus Pahl[✉]

Free University of Bozen-Bolzano, Bolzano, Italy
{shelernaz.azimi, claus.pahl}@unibz.it

Abstract. Raw source data can be made accessible in the form of processable information through Data-as-a-Service (DaaS) architectures. Machine learning is one possible way that allows to produce meaningful information and knowledge based on this raw source data. Thus, quality is a major concern that applies to raw data as well as to information provided by ML-generated models. Quality management is a major concern of AI Engineering – an attempt to systematically produce quality AI solutions. As the core of our solution, we define a conceptual framework that links input data quality and the machine learned data service quality, specifically inferring raw data problems as root causes from observed data service deficiency symptoms. This will allow to identify the hidden origins of quality problems that might be observed by users of DaaS offerings. We analyse the quality framework using a real-world case study from an edge cloud and Internet-of-Things-based traffic application. We identify quality assessment techniques for symptom and cause analysis.

Keywords: AI Engineering · Data-as-a-Service · DaaS · Machine learning · Continuous quality management · Edge cloud · Internet-of-Things · Traffic system

1 Introduction

Raw source data can be made accessible for the consumer of the service in the form of processable information through Data-as-a-Service (DaaS) architectures. A problem here is that quality concerns observed by the consumer of the service are caused by quality problems related to the raw source data or its processing – both of which are hidden from the consumer and not directly observable.

We propose an AI Engineering solution, more specifically a continuous data and machine learning (ML) model quality management in order to deal with an ongoing process of continuously monitoring and improving the quality of data and derived ML models. In particular, in contexts dominated by high volume, velocity and veracity of data (generally referred to as big data), which includes out Data-as-a-Service (DaaS) setting, this continuous quality management process is crucial. Data processing using ML techniques is an integral part of obtaining value out of the raw data, but require a dedicated quality management approach. We build on data quality models, extending the data quality concept to the ML model level. Also, we need to close the loop by

© Springer Nature Switzerland AG 2022
D. Ferguson et al. (Eds.): CLOSER 2021, CCIS 1607, pp. 69–87, 2022.
https://doi.org/10.1007/978-3-031-21637-4_4

mapping quality problems (the symptoms) at ML level back to their origins, i.e., aiming at a root cause analysis solution.

We present a layered data architecture for both data and ML function layers and enhance this by a root cause analysis based on a closed loop between two layers. We determine quality assessment mechanisms for symptom and cause analysis in different dimensions, including situational analysis and timeseries, determination outcome, object, type and techniques. Our approach is suited to situations where raw data quality might not be directly observable or assessable, thus a new way of inferring quality is needed. In order to validate our proposed solution, we use a case study. The context is a public data service (DaaS) application, specifically at a regional level (a regional IT and Data service provider). The application is traffic management, which is based on traffic and weather data collected locally in an edge cloud and IoT setting. The novelty of this paper, which extends [5], lies in the layering of data and model quality based on dedicated ML function types,

In Sect. 2, we introduce the principles of Explainable AI and AI Engineering, befre outlining the DaaS quality management framework. The details of the solution are presented in Sect. 4. In Sect. 5, we discuss the IoT traffic use case. Related work is discussed in Sect. 6 and we conclude in Sect. 7.

2   Explainable AI and AI Engineering

Explainable AI is the context of this work. Explainability is the extent to which the internal mechanics of a machine or deep learning system can be explained in human terms. Interpretability is about being able to identity the mechanics without necessarily knowing why. Explainability is being able to explain what is happening. Our ultimate objective is to automate a root cause analysis that aims to 'explain' the reasons for quality deficiencies or defects [19] in the ML model. This explains ML quality in terms of data quality [28].

Applied to our Internet-of-Things (IoT) setting, this means that for instance accuracy problems with traffic or weather prediction models or often cause by either unsuitable ML model construction or by data quality problems of data that is processed by the ML models. Here, we are specifically interested in understanding the impact of IoT data quality concerns. This in concrete terms meaning to understand if sensor failures cause incorrect readings or if network outages cause the data to be incomplete.

Overall, the aim is to move towards an explainability or interpretability of ML model failures/deficiencies as an a-posteriori measure for detection and correction [49]. Pre-construction data validation is an advisable step prior to model construction. In contrast to works in this context, we aim to identify missing values/default replacements as the root cause of prediction deficiencies (such as accuracy) as a remedial action. Some problems will still go undetected in an a pre-construction approach. Our approach (an a-posteriori analysis) can be adjusted to the presence of a-priori validation of data. Our approach also allows a black-box mode, if the construction itself is not visible/observable.

AI Engineering [7] is working towards a systematic construction of for instance ML models in order to achieve and maintain quality. Our root cause analysis can also been seen as an endeavour to continuously improve quality.

3 Continuous AI Data and Model Quality Management

3.1 Quality Principles

A continuous quality management for *data services* is a continuous process of data quality actions, namely prevention, detection and correction. The prevention of problems is, however, not always achievable. Consequently, we focus in this paper on the detection and correction of quality problems.

We target the quality of information models that are generated from data using ML techniques. Data is an asset in the IoT domain as a source for creating valuable information and knowledge. Quality is a critical requirement for the data consumer (e.g. IoT pervasive services and their users) in this context Data quality refers to how well data meets the requirements of its users. Sample aspects are accuracy, timeliness or completeness [50]. Based on this broader conceptualization and 159 defined dimensions, four main categories have been identified: Intrinsic, Contextual, Representational, Accessibility.

Quality frameworks for data and information have been investigated for a while. [3,4,34]. There is also an accepted classification of (big) data aspects that helps us in organising the quality concerns [33,42], often referred to as the *4V model*:

- volume (scale, size),
- velocity (change rate/streaming/real-time),
- variety (form/format) and
- veracity (uncertainty, accuracy, applicability).

Note, that sometimes value is added as a fifth concern, but we focus on the technical aspects here.

3.2 IoT Use Case

Our chosen IoT application domain shows all of these four main characteristics. In the *Edge Cloud* and *Internet-of-Things* (IoT), so-called things (like sensors and actuators) produce and consume data [37], processed in a edge cloud, in order to provide DaaS services.

In case the underlying data is inaccurate, any extracted information and also derived actions based on it are likely to be unreliable [27]. Thus, *data quality* concerns arise. Furthermore, the edge cloud environment in which the data collection occurs is often rapidly changing in terms of architecture and data characteristics. In order to focus our investigation, we make the following assumptions: (i) all data is numerical (i.e., text or multimedia data and corresponding quality concerns regarding formatting and syntax are not considered) and (ii) data can be stateful or stateless. Thus, IoT is a 4V big data context with specific data types, making our results transferable to similar technical environments.

The following two problems shall be addressed in our setting:

- *(1) Quality Value Analysis:* is based on quality goals and thresholds. Goals are defined in terms of quality dimensions such as accuracy or completeness. The reaching of goals is determined using predefined thresholds.

– *(2) Problem Cause Analysis and Prediction:* rely on pattern and anomaly detection to identify DaaS information model quality problems and map them the data layer, possibly including time series such as quality graphs over time (at DaaS and source data level).

The problem is if a problem source at the data layer can be identified or predicted based on an analysis of the DaaS layer, i.e., whether a root cause analysis is possible.

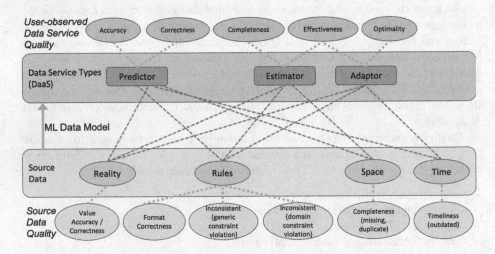

Fig. 1. A Layered DaaS quality management architecture (see [5]).

4   DaaS Quality Assessment and Problem Cause Analysis

A number of quality concerns such as accuracy or completeness have been identified in an empirical study [14] for ML data models. Our objective is to associate these concerns systematically to different root causes.

The differentiation can help to better identify IoT-level root causes for observed problems:

– *Problems with IoT input data.* Assume a data table `'TrafficCount(Location, Date/Hour, Direction1, Direction2)'`. Two types of data quality problems are: (i) missing values (e.g., for one direction), which could result from a single sensor failure, and (ii) missing record (e.g., all data for a whole hour or from one location), which could result from communication failure.
– *Problems with ML data model training.* Here unsuitable training sets (e.g., incomplete) could have been used in the construction.

4.1   Quality Layers

The starting point that forms the basis of the data quality architecture is the raw or source data layer, see Fig. 1. We can distinguish context-independent data qualities (complete, missing, duplicate, correct/accurate value, correct format, timely/outdated, inconsistent/violation of generic constraint) and context-dependent data quality (violation of domain constraints). Raw (source) data is consumed by to produce machine learning models or functions. Data concerns can be grouped:

- Reality: value accuracy and correctness - here quality concerns are gathered that can be verified against the reality,
- Rules: format correctness, consistency (generic constraints), consistency (domain constraints) - these encompass criteria usually applied to data in databases from structural/format aspects to domain-specific constraints,
- Space: completeness - this refers to completeness as a 'spacial' constraint,
- Time: timeliness - this is an attribute that indicates the timely availability of data in the system in relation to its creation time.

In order to better understand the processing purpose, we categorise these functions into DaaS function types: *predictor*, *estimator* (or calculator) and *adaptor*. For these functions, we define an information quality model. In the literature, estimation and prediction as function types are often not clearly enough distinguished. Here, we characterise them as follows [13]:

- An estimator is a rule for computing a quantity from a sample that is to be used to estimate a model parameter. An example is the average time taken for some task (for given sample). There is Low variance good (avoid noise, but can over-simplify/underfit) because of the smaller confidence interval. High variance would have a lot of detail, but miss the main feature. Guessing/estimating the main feature is desired. In comparison, there is less data, obtained in a structured, planned way (but could still be inaccurate, cf/ hospital studies). Furthermore, somewhat larger resources aids this. Generally, the main feature is fine, but any type of noise can be filtered out and simplified (but continuous and smooth). With comparably less resources, data accuracy and completeness are more of a problem. Regression is a good technique for this
- Prediction is to predict a new observation (i.e. one that is not in the sample). An example is the next predicted time another person takes to do something The point estimate (average) is probably the same, but the confidence interval (e.g. 95%) is generally wider: here there is variance on the sample and also for obtaining the new observation (value of the random variable y in one trial of an experiment, and not just to construct a confidence interval in the same sense that we have done before). Models can be discrete and jagged (rather than continuous and smooth). Low bias is good (but can do overfitting), i.e. have high precision to reduce confidence interval and be more definitive, i.e., getting a better result for the one new observation. In comparison, there is more data, but less systematically obtained (cf. image collection). Often, there is a vast amount of data, but mixed and not homogeneous. Data uncertainty (inconsistency) is more of a problem. Neural networks are good for this.

To these two widely used concepts, we add the *adaptor*:

- Adaption refers to the conversion of a prediction or estimation into an action that results from these. The difference to the previous two is that the quality concern is effectiveness of the action, not the predicted or estimated value. What is measured is how well the action remedies any undesired predicted or estimated value. Optimising effectiveness rather than accuracy is the main quality objective of this function. An example is a controller that manages the workload of a machine. Machine configuration parameters can by (if necessary, dynamically) reconfigured through the calculated action in order to optimise the productivity.

The evaluation of our use case will shows that we can relate DaaS function quality to DaaS function types and techniques, see Fig. 1: Predictors are concerned with accuracy (regression) and correctness (classification). Estimator are concerned with effectiveness (clustering) and completeness (clustering). Adaptors are concerned with effectiveness (classification) and optimality (regression). Input for function quality includes thus the following aspects:

- structural model quality: accuracy, correctness, completeness, effectivess, optimality and
- function-specific quality: accuracy/correctness (for the predictor), complete/ effective (for the estimator), effectiveness/optimality (for the adaptor).

Furthermore ethical model/function quality includes fairness, privacy-preserving. Note, that is essential here to assess the quality of the function provided by the ML models, which emerge in different types, such as predictors, estimators or adaptors. Often multiple goals involved. For example, primary goal effective (performance threshold) with secondary goal optimality (energy/resources) to maintain the threshold.

4.2 MAPE-K Service Quality Loop

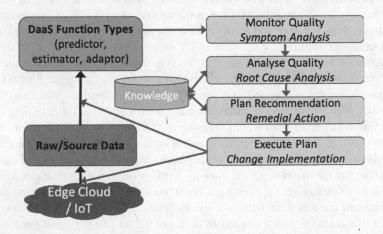

Fig. 2. Closed service feedback quality loop based on the MAPE-K pattern (see [5]).

The quality management for our DaaS architecture includes a feedback loop based on the MAPE-K adaptation pattern (with its Knowledge-based phases Monitor, Analyse,

Plan and Execute) to control data and information quality, see Fig. 2. At the core is a mapping of DaaS model quality to source data quality based Fig. 1 presented earlier.

We start with accuracy, which is often considered the most important quality concern. High precision relates to a low false positive (FP) rate

$$TP/(TP+FP)$$

i.e., correctly identified over incorrectly identified. High recall relates to a low false negative (FN) rate

$$TP/(TP+FN)$$

i.e., correctly identified over not identified correct cases. High precision means that a DaaS function returns substantially more relevant results than irrelevant ones, while high recall means that it returns most of the relevant results. Correctness plays a significant role in this function.

Influencing factors for *predictor accuracy* are data incompleteness, data incorrectness, data duplication, and outdated data. An example is the count of road services per areas, which could suffer from outdated or duplicated data. For correctness, the same observations apply. For *estimator effectiveness*, an example is outdated date, which applies to self-adaptive systems for traffic control that directly depend on the current situation. *Adaptor ineffectiveness* could be caused by an incorrect format in temperature measurements (Celsius vs Fahrenheit). Some of these conditions, as in the 'outdated' case, also depend on whether the application context is stateful or stateless .

An analysis of data quality problems for an observed ML quality problem could lead to remediation recommendations [15, 16] in two categories: *Source data:* recommendation to use other raw/source data, which could mean more, different, or less data. *ML training/testing data:* recommendation to use other ML training/testing data selected or to use even another ML technique. These would ideally be automatically derived.

5   An IoT-Edge Traffic Management Use Case

We look now at quality assessment and symptom analysis activities.

5.1   Quality and Symptom Analysis

We identified different DaaS functions earlier that shall be looked at in terms of (1) the quality dimension and its definition, (2) a concrete example of a DaaS function and (3) the determination of quality value. In a negative quality case, we refer to the symptom. These are based on a vehicle data set based on the 'TrafficCount', combined with 'WeatherData' for the respective location, see Fig. 3. We need to consider how quality is measured and how success is determined. We distinguish the three function types and their quality goals. The functions and their expected qualities are summarised in Table 1.

1. An *estimator* for traffic volume has the following concerns: effective and complete. Effectiveness can be defined as to what extend the estimation can be correct and

#	SITI_CODSI TO	RILV_IDENT NR	DATAORA	CANALE	DIREZIONE	VALORE	SCHEMAVE LOCITA	SCHEMACL ASSE
1	00000002	1878212	31JAN2018:06:00:00	1	2	1	26	2
2	00000002	1878212	31JAN2018:06:00:00	1	2	1	14	2
3	00000002	1878212	31JAN2018:06:00:00	1	2	1	15	6
4	00000002	1878212	31JAN2018:06:00:00	1	2	1	15	7
5	00000002	1878212	31JAN2018:06:00:00	1	2	1	16	2
6	00000002	1878212	31JAN2018:06:00:00	1	2	1	16	4
7	00000002	1878212	31JAN2018:06:00:00	1	2	1	16	5
8	00000002	1878212	31JAN2018:06:00:00	1	2	1	16	8
9	00000002	1878212	31JAN2018:06:00:00	1	2	23	17	2
10	00000002	1878212	31JAN2018:06:00:00	1	2	3	17	4
11	00000002	1878212	31JAN2018:06:00:00	1	2	3	17	5
12	00000002	1878212	31JAN2018:06:00:00	1	2	6	17	6
13	00000002	1878212	31JAN2018:06:00:00	1	2	1	17	7
14	00000002	1878212	31JAN2018:06:00:00	1	2	1	17	8
15	00000002	1878212	31JAN2018:06:00:00	1	2	47	18	2
16	00000002	1878212	31JAN2018:06:00:00	1	2	7	18	4
17	00000002	1878212	31JAN2018:06:00:00	1	2	4	18	5

Fig. 3. Traffic count data set - based on regional recordings https://mobility.api.opendatahub.bz. it/v2/swagger-ui.html - (see [5]).

effective for better performance. For example, to estimate the traffic volume for an August in general irrespective of concrete weather, we obtain the result by using supervised learning. To ensure the correctness of the estimation, the historic data should be checked, e.g., the results from earlier years $Y1$ and $Y2$ imply the estimation year $Y3$, i.e., $Y1, Y2 \rightarrow Y3$. This function is used for *long-term road planning* for all roads, see Fig. 3. Completeness for the estimator is easy to calculate.

2. A *predictor* for traffic volume and level for a concrete future date is the second function.

Fig. 4. Public DaaS [Web Site] – Traffic level prediction – motivated by https://www. autobrennero.it/en/on-the-road/traffic-forecast/ - (see [5]).

The function calculates a volume V using $F(T,C,W) \rightarrow V : INT$ based on temperature, number of cars and weekday. For immediate assessment, we need to check observations in the current state and assume problems might have been there also in the past. Furthermore, we cannot predict the likelihood of any source of problem. As another example, we can consider a predictor for car types: accurate and correct. In this situation correctness can be considered a special case of accuracy, that is 100% accuracy in this situation. This function is used for *short/mid-term management* on major roads as exemplified in Fig. 4.

3. An *adaptor* for traffic signs has effectiveness and optimality as concerns.

Fig. 5. Public DaaS [Road Sign] – dynamic traffic signpost on the motorway - (see [5]).

Contrary to estimators and predictors, an adaptor also proposes some actions after the calculation and evaluation of the situation. An adaptor function should be effective. For this function the calculations for speed are done based on car volume and emissions ($F(C,E) = Speed$). The optimal target is minimal emissions E_{min}, but this is constrained by traffic throughput (too restrictive speed limit might cause traffic stop and thus low emissions, but throughput is inadequate). The evaluations are done by checking whether the goals are achieved or not. This is used for example for *immediate motorway management*, see Fig. 5. If the quality is insufficient, the problem could be either the training data and sensors.

Table 1. Use Cases – DaaS functions and quality (see [5]).

	(1) Estimator	(2) Predictor	(3) Adaptor
Function & Quality	Estimator: effective, complete	Predictor: accurate, correct	Adaptor: effective
Sample Function	estimate the traffic volume for an August in general	car type categorisation	calculate traffic sign action (target: change speed limits to lower emissions)
Quality Value	*Calculation*: correctness of prediction for historic data (could use for training/validation data from past August or previous July). *Success*: degree of effectiveness for threshold T	*Calculation*: Precision, Recall based on *TP, FP, FP, FN*. *Success*: a threshold T on predefined degree of accuracy.	*Calculation*: observation after applying action $OBS_E(Apply(Action))$. *Success*: is effective, if $E_{i+1} < E_i$ for emissions E. The aim is the reach a target emission while not having too slow traffic.

5.2   Root Cause Analysis and Remedial Action Recommendation

The root cause analysis shall be looked at in more detail. The use cases are summarised in the respective tables for the data quality analysis and for the problem root cause analysis and recommendation.

For all cases, we note (i) calculation of metric, (ii) assessment of problem situation, (iii) analysis of possible root causes (along the two categories or more fine-granular in terms of concrete data quality dimensions, and (iv) a strategy for better cause determination. The aim is now to determine a cause (either definitive or likely) from sources such as training data or source data.

The three main steps hall be presented in the next subsections.

5.3   Step 1 Metric Calculation and Step 2 Problem Assessment

These steps are presented in Table 2. For the predictor accuracy, we analysed the accuracy input parameters:

- *TP:* if the current state $OBS(currentstate)$ is correct and the next state

$$V = OBS(nextstate)$$

  also results in correctness – indicates a given condition exists, when it really does.
- *FP:* if current state $OBS(currentstate)$ is incorrect and next state

$$V = OBS(nextstate)$$

  results in correctness – indicates a given condition exists, when it does not.
- *TN:* if current state $OBS(currentstate)$ is correct and next state

$$V \neq OBS(nextstate)$$

  results in incorrectness – indicates a condition does not hold, when it really does not.
- *FN:* if current state $OBS(currentstate)$ is incorrect and next state

$$V \neq OBS(nextstate)$$

  results in incorrectness – indicates that a condition does not hold, while in fact it does hold.

5.4   Step 3 – Root Cause Analysis and Recommendation

Table 2 presents the use case. For Case 2 for example, false positive (FP) is an error in data reporting, in which a result improperly indicates a problem, when in reality it is not present. More concretely, this could be a vehicle that is not a car, but incorrectly recognised as one. A false negative (FN) is an error in which a result wrongly indicates no quality problem (the result is negative), when actually it is present. Here, raw sensor data can be wrong, e.g., sensors giving incomplete data (such as too small dimensions given) so that a van is recognised as a car) or training data is wrong. For the latter case, e.g., not enough annotated/labelled cars are in the training set so that very large cars (SUV) are identified as a van or truck.

Table 2. Use Cases – DaaS quality analysis (see [5]).

	(1) Estimator	(2) Predictor	(3) Adaptor
Calculation of Metric	$F(C,P) \rightarrow Volume$ estimates volumes of traffic for general periods	$F(T,C,W) \rightarrow Volume$ predicts vehicle numbers based on temperature, counted cars, weekday	$F(C,E) = Speed$ adapts speed limits based on car volume and emission
Assessment of Problem Situation	Goal achievement: – the results from earlier years $Y1$ to $Y2$ imply the estimation $Y3$, i.e., $Y1, \ldots, Y2 \rightarrow Y3$	Goal achievement: – Four cases occur: (i) 100% accuracy, (ii) < 100% accuracy, but within tolerance (threshold T), (iii) $< T\%$, (iv) undefined. – Accuracy is defined using $Precision = \frac{TP}{TP+FP}$ and $Recall = \frac{TP}{TP+FN}$	Goal achievement: – emissions (primary): $E_{new} \leq E_T$ for threshold T as ultimate goal; $E_{new} < E_{old}$ as just improvement, i.e. these are 100% effective, and x% effective. – throughput: $OBS_C($ $Apply(\ Speed)) =$ C_{new} – secondary: C_{new} as close as possible to C_{old}

Based on these observations, FP problem causes are as follows:

– raw data is wrong: e.g., sensors giving incomplete data such as too small dimensions given so that a van is recognised as a car,
– training data is wrong: e.g., not enough annotated/labelled cars in training set so that very large cars (SUV) are identified as vans/trucks.

Similarly, the FN problem causes can also be summarised:

– raw data wrong: either sensors giving incomplete data (e.g., too big dimensions provided, so that its recognised as a van) or sensors giving incomplete data (e.g., too small dimensions given so that a van is recognised as a car),
– training (data) wrong: not enough annotated/labelled cars in training set so that very large cars (SUV) are identified as van/truck training (data) wrong (not enough annotated/labelled cars in training set so that very small or very large cars are not covered.

Root Cause Analysis. Problems can be identified by searching for indicative patterns or anomalies. In pattern identification different situations can be distinguished.

For example, a steep decrease in a quality graph over time (time series) could point to a sudden sensor failure. A gradual decrease of quality could point to problems within the data. In a flat effectiveness quality graph, the problem could be arising from the training data. Or in other cases, in a classification function, patterns in sequences of symbols can have different meanings in each situation, e.g., unexpected repeated symbols or unexpected increase in symbols. Examples where *time series* can help are firstly *outages*, i.e., no data for a period (communications problem), and secondly *incorrect data*, i.e., sensors faulty (e.g., giving to high measurements). Here, the Assessment is based on the detection of patterns or anomalies.

A time series for a current assessment could for example be a normal series $CBTCBT$, changing into $CCTTCC$ as a sequence that shows an unusual pattern (here for vehicle categories car C, bike B and truck T). The cause analysis uses pattern/anomaly detection, with pattern mappings to the data level. Time series can be used for predictive maintenance, i.e., through the identification of changing patterns can predict a future problem.

Remedial Action Recommendation. A strategy generally used in quality remediation is training data validation. Different DaaS functions F_i are created for different training data sets and then according to the result different options can be taken.

One option is to compare functions themselves and another one is to compare input/output values. For instance, we could do majority vote on similarity (e.g., on 3 data sets). If one is different, this set has a specific property, e.g., more July data than others. The recommendation could be to check July data for completeness or accuracy. This might have to be done manually. If necessary, a different function needs to be constructed.

In this context, the primary remedial strategy is starting with training data changes and/or constructing different DaaS functions. An automated comparison can then be carried out, in relation to historic data or between different functions.

5.5 Transferability

We looked at IoT settings, based on sensors as data producers. In that context, we have used traffic and weather data sets.

We considered these two domains – traffic management and weather – so far as examples of discrete numeric data. Another application domain is mobile learning that equally includes heavy use of data being collected from and delivered to mobile learners and their devices and includes the usage of multimedia content being delivered to mobile learners and their devices [20,21,29,31,36]. These systems also rely on close interaction with semantic processing of interactions in order to support cognitive learning processes [15,18], which would help to increase the understandability of the DaaS offering provided. Here the setting is different in that multimedia content is produced and transferred. This can equally cause incompleteness and incorrectness problems, but here the differences is that continuous streams of binary data is affected.

A further direction is the implementation of self-adaptive ML quality management in an IoT-edge continuum [24,30]. In that context, similar to the original setting, sensors produce data (albeit sensors measuring often virtualized infrastructure performance) that is after some analysed translated into instructions to be executed by actuators in the same IoT edge space. Here, video surveillance could be considered, where cameras monitor for example building that need protection. Image quality could be monitored and faults in the video or transmission system detected. Microservices and containers [35,39,47,48] would here be the main artifacts that would be monitored, causing continuously produced input data.

From our results, we can ascertain that sensor faults have a different impact than for instance network failures and that with some certainty a defect cause can be identified. This, however, needs to be further explored and confirmed for other data than the numerical and limited volume situations considered here.

6 Related Work

In our review of related work, we look at the data quality level, machine learning process perspective and DaaS model quality. Data-level quality has been considered in [34], [10], [44]. In [34], data quality problems have been classified into two groups of context-independent and context-dependant distinguished by the data and user perspective. In [10], an architecture based on Blockchain technology has been proposed to improve data quality and false data detection. In [44], a cross-domain prototype of a lightweight distributed architecture for IoT was also presented, providing supporting algorithms for the assessment of data quality and security. In order to adapt to our IoT application context, we build on [34].

A machine learning workflow with nine stages was presented in [2], where the early stages are data oriented. Generally, workflows connected to ML are non-linear and often contain several feedback loops to earlier stages. If a system contains multiple machine learning components, that interact together in complex and unexpected ways, this type of workflow can become complex. Our aim is to investigate here as a novel perspective a broader loop from the later final ML function stages to the initial data and ML training configuration stages. There is also work specific to the machine learning layer, such as [40] and [9]. There, different supervised learning approaches were used. They noted that different methods have different applications. They analysed in this context the effect of calibrating these models via Platt scaling and isotonic regression on their performance as a quality concern.

Specific quality metrics applied to ML-based data models have been investigated. FOr instance, [22] discusses the area under the receiver operating characteristic curve (AUC) as a sample quality for classification models. In [46], a solution for model governance in production machine learning is introduced where provenance information and be traced demonstration the emergence of an ML prediction solution. Also the quality of data in ML has been looked at. An application use case was presented there, but without a systematic coverage of quality aspects.

Data quality is important in many ML-supported DaaS applications, such as scientific computing. In [12], a high-energy physics experiment as an IoT-type setting is investigated, which demonstrates the need for a systematic, automated approach to achieve a higher level of accuracy compared to training problems arising from manual data labelling. In [11] another IoT and edge cloud setting.is considered that emphasises the uncertainty of sensory data as the main problem causes. Their proposal is to give data quality a crucial role in this process. [14] is related to our setting, but only covers IoT root causes in the analysis, but does not cover ML training data problems. Our aim is to condense different individual quality concerns in a single quality model for DaaS data services that takes on board lessons learned from [11, 12, 14], but also closed feedback loop as we indicated in our architecture model.

In [45], the authors employed three supervised machine learning (ML) algorithms, Bayesian Networks, Decision Trees and Multilayer Perceptrons for the flow-based classification of six different types of Internet traffic including peer-to-peer(P2P) and content delivery (Akamai) traffic. They investigated the dependency of the traffic classification performance on the amount and composition of training data. They also showed that ML algorithms such as Bayesian Networks and Decision Trees are suitable for Internet traffic flow classification at a high speed and proved to be robust with respect to applications that dynamically change their source ports.

[25] and [6] employed machine learning methods to improve accuracy. Improving the data accuracy and reliability is one of our main goals which makes these papers a good reference for us that provide accuracy specific quality improvement strategies. In [8] a survey of data mining applications in business is provided to investigate the use of learning techniques. [32] provides an overview of the application of ML to optical communications and networking. [26] proposes a deep learning method that combines CNN and LSTM to detect abnormal network traffic, especially unknown intrusions. In [2], nine stages were specified for a ML workflow in which some of the stages were data oriented. ML workflows are highly non-linear and contain several feedback loops which may loop back to any previous stage. This workflow can become even more complex if the system is integrative, containing multiple ML components which interact together. [2, 8, 26, 32] have all presented useful background and information on how to use machine learning for different purposes and in different applications. All this information is needed for us in order to use machine learning and investigate specific quality concerns in our case study application.

The machine learning model layer has been studied in [40] and [9]. Different algorithms and approaches were introduced and used in these papers which were mostly building on supervised learning algorithms. They also examined the effect that calibrating the models via Platt scaling and isotonic regression has on their performances and quality. [1] introduced an automated secure continuous cloud service availability framework for smart connected vehicles that enables an intrusion detection mechanism against security attacks and provides services that meet users' quality of service (QoS) and quality of experience (QoE) requirements.

Intrusion detection is accomplished through a three-phase data traffic analysis, reduction, and classification technique used to identify positive trusted service requests against false requests that may occur during intrusion attacks. The solution adopts deep belief and decision tree machine learning mechanisms used for data reduction and classification purposes, respectively. The framework is validated through simulations to demonstrate the effectiveness of the solution in terms of intrusion attack detection. We plan to expand what the authors in this paper did for our project. This is a relevant example of how to improve machine learning model quality. The papers in this section mostly investigate new methods for a better accuracy in data using different machine learning methods.

Table 3. DaaS quality assessment dimensions (see [5]).

	DaaS quality value		
Quality value	Accuracy	Correct/ effective:	Optimal
Metric & measurement	Mostly done manual, maybe automated with other sensors, e.g., optical issues (dust) or loss of connectivity can be detected	Historic data – can be mostly automated	Can be automated, but needs waiting for the next state; can either be ML data or raw data

Table 4. DaaS quality assessment dimensions (see [5]).

	DaaS quality time series		
Quality value	Accuracy	Correct/effective	Optimal
Metric & Measurement	Determine source by mapping time series to underlying raw data sequences (e.g., car type series)	Temperature prediction series (jump > 20 degrees is sensor fault)	Time series could be difficult to interpret (if heating switched on or cloud workload is suddenly high), the adaptor will struggle

The quality of data in a machine learning approach has been investigated in [14], where an application use case is presented that identifies relevant data quality concerns in an IoT setting. A systematic coverage of quality aspects, is however not attempted. [17,41] discusses the ensuring of fairness in machine learning to advance health equity which is a concern that is different from the usual accuracy.

7   Conclusions

The aim of data processing solution is to make data accessible that in its original source data format would not be useful to a consumer. Machine learning is often used to process this data in order to create meaningful information for the final DaaS consumer. Normally, accuracy is the key objective of the created data models, but we aim here at a broader categorisation of qualities, covering the source data as well as the ML-based DaaS model layer. We presented here an integrated DaaS quality management framework. We provided a fine-granular model for a range of service quality concerns addressing common types of machine learning function types such as predictors, estimators and adaptors.

The central technical contribution of our paper is the mapping of observable quality deficiencies of DaaS functions to underlying, possibly hidden data quality problems. Providing a root cause analysis for symptoms observed by the service consumer is the objective. In addition, remedial actions for the identified problems and their causes can be proposed to the user by the solution.

We validated of both DaaS function types and related data quality types in symptom and root cause analysis through use cases. In our IoT and edge cloud case study, quality data regarding current situations and also time series have been addressed. Furthermore, *aggregation* is a mechanism based on location or time, but, this has not been covered in our use cases. Both situational and time series-based quality analysis have been covered in Tables 3 and 4, respectively.

As part of our future work, some open concerns shall be addressed. We have introduced here informal definitions for function and data quality, but these still need to be formalised in our framework. Furthermore, we will also deal with more complex settings with multiple clusters of data producers that would need to be coordinated, following our earlier work on these architectures [16,23,24,43]. Thus work would allow us to generalise the results to multiple data services [38] in an edge cloud setting. A final concern is root cause identification, e.g., basing this on the analysis of ML techniques like regression, classification or clustering. Also statistical/probabilistic models such as Markov Models can be used to map observable data processing function quality to hidden data quality.

Acknowledgements. This work has been performed partly within a Ph.D. Programme funded through a bursary by the Südtiroler Informatik AG (SIAG).

References

1. Aloqaily, M., Otoum, S., Al Ridhawi, I., Jararweh, Y.: An intrusion detection system for connected vehicles in smart cities. Ad Hoc Netw. **90**, 101842 (2019). https://doi.org/10.1016/j.adhoc.2019.02.001
2. Amershi, S., et al.: Software engineering for machine learning: a case study. In: Intl Conf on Software Engineering - Software Engineering in Practice track. IEEE (2019). https://www.microsoft.com/en-us/research/publication/software-engineering-for-machine-learning-a-case-study/
3. Azimi, S., Pahl, C.: A layered quality framework in machine learning driven data and information models. In: 22nd International Conference on Enterprise Information Systems (2020)
4. Azimi, S., Pahl, C.: Root cause analysis and remediation for quality and value improvement in machine learning driven information models. In: 22nd International Conference on Enterprise Information Systems (2020)
5. Azimi, S., Pahl, C.: Continuous data quality management for machine learning based data-as-a-service architectures. In: International Conference on Cloud Computing and Services Science CLOSER (2021)
6. Bermolen, P., Mellia, M., Meo, M., Rossi, D., Valenti, S.: Abacus: accurate behavioral classification of p2p-tv traffic. Comput. Netw. **55**(6), 1394–1411 (2011)
7. Bosch, J., Olsson, H.H., Crnkovic, I.: Engineering ai systems: a research agenda. In: Artificial Intelligence Paradigms for Smart Cyber-Physical Systems, pp. 1–19. IGI Global (2021)
8. Bose, I., Mahapatra, R.: Business data mining - a machine learning perspective. Inf. Manag. **39**, 211–225 (2001). https://doi.org/10.1016/S0378-7206(01)00091-X
9. Caruana, R., Niculescu-Mizil, A.: An empirical comparison of supervised learning algorithms. In: Proceedings of the 23rd International Conference on Machine Learning, pp. 161–168 (2006)

10. Casado-Vara, R., de la Prieta, F., Prieto, J., Corchado, J.M.: Blockchain framework for IoT data quality via edge computing. In: Proceedings of the 1st Workshop on Blockchain-Enabled Networked Sensor Systems, pp. 19–24 (2018)
11. De Hoog, J., Mercelis, S., Hellinckx, P.: Improving machine learning-based decision-making through inclusion of data quality. In: CEUR Workshop Proceedings, vol. 2491 (2019)
12. Deja, K.: Using machine learning techniques for data quality monitoring in CMS and ALICE. In: Proceedings of Science, vol. 350 (2019)
13. Efron, B.: Prediction, estimation, and attribution. J. Am. Stat. Assoc. **115**(530), 636–655 (2020). https://doi.org/10.1080/01621459.2020.1762613
14. Ehrlinger, L., Haunschmid, V., Palazzini, D., Lettner, C.: A DaQL to monitor data quality in machine learning applications. In: Hartmann, S., Küng, J., Chakravarthy, S., Anderst-Kotsis, G., Tjoa, A.M., Khalil, I. (eds.) DEXA 2019. LNCS, vol. 11706, pp. 227–237. Springer, Cham (2019). https://doi.org/10.1007/978-3-030-27615-7_17
15. Fang, D., Liu, X., Romdhani, I., Jamshidi, P., Pahl, C.: An agility-oriented and fuzziness-embedded semantic model for collaborative cloud service search, retrieval and recommendation. Future Gener. Comput. Syst. **56**, 11–26 (2016)
16. Fowley, F., Pahl, C., Jamshidi, P., Fang, D., Liu, X.: A classification and comparison framework for cloud service brokerage architectures. IEEE Trans. Cloud Comput. **6**(2), 358–371 (2018)
17. Gu, L., Zeng, D., Guo, S., Barnawi, A., Xiang, Y.: Cost efficient resource management in fog computing supported medical cyber-physical system. IEEE Trans. Emerg. Top. Comput. **5**(1), 108–119 (2017). https://doi.org/10.1109/TETC.2015.2508382
18. Javed, M., Abgaz, Y.M., Pahl, C.: Ontology change management and identification of change patterns. J. Data Semant. **2**(2–3), 119–143 (2013). https://doi.org/10.1007/s13740-013-0024-2
19. Jiarpakdee, J., Tantithamthavorn, C., Dam, H.K., Grundy, J.: An empirical study of model-agnostic techniques for defect prediction models. In: IEEE Transactions on Software Engineering, pp. 1–1 (2020)
20. Kenny, C., Pahl, C.: Automated tutoring for a database skills training environment. In: 36th Technical Symposium on Computer Science Education, SIGCSE, pp. 58–62. ACM (2005). https://doi.org/10.1145/1047344.1047377
21. Kenny, C., Pahl, C.: Automated tutoring for a database skills training environment. In: Proceedings of the 36th SIGCSE Technical Symposium on Computer Science Education, pp. 58–62. SIGCSE '05, Association for Computing Machinery, New York, NY, USA (2005). https://doi.org/10.1145/1047344.1047377
22. Kleiman, R., Page, D.: Auc μ: a performance metric for multi-class machine learning models. In: International Conference on Machine Learning, pp. 3439–3447 (2019)
23. von Leon, D., Miori, L., Sanin, J., Ioini, N.E., Helmer, S., Pahl, C.: A performance exploration of architectural options for a middleware for decentralised lightweight edge cloud architectures. In: International Conference on Internet of Things, Big Data and Security, pp. 73–84 (2018). https://doi.org/10.5220/0006677400730084
24. von Leon, D., Miori, L., Sanin, J., Ioini, N.E., Helmer, S., Pahl, C.: A lightweight container middleware for edge cloud architectures. In: Fog and Edge Computing, pp. 145–170. Wiley Series on Parallel and Distributed Computing, Wiley (2019). https://doi.org/10.1002/9781119525080.ch7
25. Li, W., Moore, A.: A machine learning approach for efficient traffic classification, pp. 310–317 (2007). https://doi.org/10.1109/MASCOTS.2007.2
26. Lu, X., Liu, P., Lin, J.: Network traffic anomaly detection based on information gain and deep learning, pp. 11–15 (2019). https://doi.org/10.1145/3325917.3325946

27. Mahdavinejad, M.S., Rezvan, M., Barekatain, M., Adibi, P., Barnaghi, P., Sheth, A.P.: Machine learning for internet of things data analysis: a survey. Digital Commun. Netw. **4**(3), 161–175 (2018)

28. Marev, M.S., Compatangelo, E., Vasconcelos, W.W.: Towards a context-dependent numerical data quality evaluation framework. CoRR abs/1810.09399 (2018). https://arxiv.org/abs/1810.09399

29. Melia, M., Pahl, C.: Constraint-based validation of adaptive e-learning courseware. IEEE Trans. Learn. Technol. **2**(1), 37–49 (2009)

30. Mendonça, N.C., Jamshidi, P., Garlan, D., Pahl, C.: Developing self-adaptive microservice systems: challenges and directions. IEEE Softw. **38**(2), 70–79 (2021)

31. Murray, S., Ryan, J., Pahl, C.: Tool-mediated cognitive apprenticeship approach for a computer engineering course. In: International Conference on Advanced Learning Technologies, pp. 2–6. IEEE (2003). https://doi.org/10.1109/ICALT.2003.1215014

32. Musumeci, F., et al.: An overview on application of machine learning techniques in optical networks. IEEE Commun. Surv. Tutorials **21**(2), 1383–1408 (2019)

33. Nguyen, T.L.: A framework for five big v's of big data and organizational culture in firms. In: International Conference on Big Data (2018)

34. O'Brien, T., Helfert, M., Sukumar, A.: The value of good data- a quality perspective a framework and discussion. In: International Conference on Enterprise Information Systems (2013)

35. Pahl, C.: An ontology for software component matching. In: Pezzè, M. (ed.) FASE 2003. LNCS, vol. 2621, pp. 6–21. Springer, Heidelberg (2003). https://doi.org/10.1007/3-540-36578-8_2

36. Pahl, C., Barrett, R., Kenny, C.: Supporting active database learning and training through interactive multimedia. In: 9th Conference on Innovation and Technology in Computer Science Education, ITiCSE, pp. 27–31. ACM (2004). https://doi.org/10.1145/1007996.1008007

37. Pahl, C., Fronza, I., Ioini, N.E., Barzegar, H.R.: A review of architectural principles and patterns for distributed mobile information systems. In: International Conference on Web Information Systems and Technologies (2019)

38. Pahl, C., Ioini, N.E., Helmer, S., Lee, B.A.: An architecture pattern for trusted orchestration in IoT edge clouds. In: International Conference on Fog and Mobile Edge Computing. IEEE (2018). https://doi.org/10.1109/FMEC.2018.8364046

39. Pahl, C., Jamshidi, P., Zimmermann, O.: Microservices and containers. Softw. Eng. **2020** (2020)

40. Plewczynski, D., Spieser, S.A.H., Koch, U.: Assessing different classification methods for virtual screening. J. Chem. Inf. Model. **46**(3), 1098–1106 (2006)

41. Rajkomar, A., Hardt, M., Howell, M.D., Corrado, G., Chin, M.H.: Ensuring fairness in machine learning to advance health equity. Annals Intern. Med. **169**(12), 866–872 (2018)

42. Saha, B., Srivastava, D.: Data quality: the other face of big data. In: 2014 IEEE 30th International Conference on Data Engineering, pp. 1294–1297. IEEE (2014)

43. Scolati, R., Fronza, I., Ioini, N.E., Samir, A., Pahl, C.: A containerized big data streaming architecture for edge cloud computing on clustered single-board devices. In: International Conference on Cloud Computing and Services Science (2019). https://doi.org/10.5220/0007695000680080

44. Sicari, S., Rizzardi, A., Miorandi, D., Cappiello, C., Coen-Porisini, A.: A secure and quality-aware prototypical architecture for the internet of things. Inf. Syst. **58**, 43–55 (2016)

45. Soysal, M., Schmidt, E.G.: Machine learning algorithms for accurate flow-based network traffic classification: evaluation and comparison. Perform. Eval. **67**(6), 451–467 (2010)

46. Sridhar, V., Subramanian, S., Arteaga, D., Sundararaman, S., Roselli, D.S., Talagala, N.: Model governance: reducing the anarchy of production ml. In: USENIX Annual Technical Conference (2018)

47. Taibi, D., Lenarduzzi, V., Pahl, C.: Continuous architecting with microservices and devops: a systematic mapping study. In: Muñoz, V.M., Ferguson, D., Helfert, M., Pahl, C. (eds.) CLOSER 2018. CCIS, vol. 1073, pp. 126–151. Springer, Cham (2019). https://doi.org/10.1007/978-3-030-29193-8_7
48. Taibi, D., Lenarduzzi, V., Pahl, C., Janes, A.: Microservices in agile software development: a workshop-based study into issues, advantages, and disadvantages. In: Proceedings of the XP2017 Scientific Workshops, pp. 1–5 (2017)
49. Tantithamthavorn, C., Jiarpakdee, J., Grundy, J.: Explainable AI for software engineering. arXiv preprint. arXiv:2012.01614 (2020)
50. Thatipamula, S.: Data done right: 6 dimensions of data quality. https://smartbridge.com/data-done-right-6-dimensions-of-data-quality/ (2013). Accessed 16 Jan 2021

Quality of Service Support Through a Self-adaptive System in Edge Computing Environments

Abdullah Fawaz Aljulayfi[1,2]([✉]) [iD] and Karim Djemame[1] [iD]

[1] School of Computing, University of Leeds, Leeds, UK
{ml16afa, K.Djemame}@Leeds.ac.uk
[2] Prince Sattam Bin Abdulaziz University, Al-Kharj, Saudi Arabia

Abstract. Edge Computing (EC) has gained a lot of attention from both industry and academia as it is an essential paradigm that addresses the Quality of Service (QoS) of Internet of Things (IoT) applications. The QoS metrics are defined in a Service Level Agreement (SLA) that must be fulfilled by Service Provider (SP). Indeed, the management of QoS in EC is not a trivial process due to the dynamicity nature of both EC and IoT devices as well as the IoT applications' requirements. This rises the need to develop a Self-adaptive System (SAS) that is aware of IoT- and EC-nature and provides a continuous management over the operation environment with consideration to the optimization objectives. Self-adaptation is seen as a promising method to manage such objectives in an efficient manner. In this paper, a QoS framework embedded in a SAS is proposed with respect to the EC environment in terms of workload fluctuation and limited resources. Its design also evaluated using a comprehensive simulation-based investigation that considers the most suitable scheduling algorithm, resource threshold, and resource monitoring interval. The simulation results show that the considered parameters can significantly improve the targeted objectives, which can be up to ~35% and more than 50% in acceptance rate and processing time, respectively. Such improvement is related to understanding the relationship among these parameters and the adopted workload.

Keywords: Edge computing · Internet of Things · Quality of Service · Self-adaptive system · Elasticity · Proactive · Reactive · Hybrid · Autonomic computing

1 Introduction

Over the last few years, Edge Computing (EC) paradigm has attracted the attention of both academia and industry duo to its potential role in promoting Internet of Thing (IoT) applications [1, 2]. It brings the centralized Cloud Computing (CC) services as utility computing closer to the data source at the network's periphery aiming to fulfill the IoT requirements, such as mobility support, low latency, and reliability [3, 4]. These requirements formalize the Quality of Service (QoS) metrics that are specified by the

© Springer Nature Switzerland AG 2022
D. Ferguson et al. (Eds.): CLOSER 2021, CCIS 1607, pp. 88–114, 2022.
https://doi.org/10.1007/978-3-031-21637-4_5

Service Consumer (SC) (i.e., IoT devices) in a formal contract known as Service Level Agreement (SLA) [5, 6]. The SLA is used to specify the minimum service performance requirements that must be fulfilled by the Service Provider (SP) (i.e., EC owner) [7].

Despite of the phenomenal performance provided by EC to address the SC requirements, it still suffers from several challenges that augment the complexity of QoS management. These challenges are threefold. The first challenge is the nature of EC which represents a bottleneck in QoS management process as EC infrastructure consists of geo-distributed and heterogeneous nodes [8], has limited resources [9], and can operate in a low power environment [10]. The IoT devices properties are also considered as a major challenge as the number of these devices has increased massively and expected to be more than 27 billion devices by 2025 [11]. Further, its workload is highly dynamic and fluctuating due to e.g., user mobility. Another challenge is the conflicting optimization objectives that needs to be managed by the SP. In one hand, IoT devices have specific objectives defined in SLA. On the other hand, SP also has optimization objectives, such as energy consumption minimization and revenue maximization as well as efficient resource utilization. The objective's confliction makes the QoS management even more complex.

This complexity raises the need to adopt autonomic computing which can be provided through a Self-adaptive System (SAS) that considers EC nature, SP optimization concerns, QoS metrics, and IoT devices dynamicity. SAS is a promising solution that provides a full autonomic management for QoS provision and specified objectives [12]. This paper builds on our previous work [13] which proposes a high level SAS architecture that contains elasticity- and QoS-framework. The elasticity framework is designed and evaluated in [14], where the proactive side that utilizes Machine Learning (ML) models is proposed and evaluated in [15].

The previous work is extended in this paper by designing a QoS framework embedded in SAS that supports the applications' QoS in terms of low latency, which is SC objective, as well as the acceptance rate maximization, whereby it is a SP objective. Moreover, its design involves a comprehensive simulation-based investigation to select the most suitable task scheduling algorithms, resource utilization threshold, and resource monitoring interval for EC environment and IoT workload.

The contributions of this paper are:

- A novel QoS framework including its underlying algorithms, namely, QoS manager and admission control, are proposed; such framework considers conflicting objectives, which are low latency as SC objective and acceptance rate maximization as SP objectives.
- A thorough evaluation on the performance of the proposed framework is performed; this evaluation also considers the task scheduling algorithms, resource utilization threshold, and resource monitoring interval aiming to find the most suitable algorithm, threshold, and monitoring interval for the EC environments.
- The relationship between the selected evaluation metrics and workload is studied; such analysis provides some recommendations accordingly.

The rest of this paper is organized as follows. Section 2 presents the related work. This is followed by Sect. 3 which describes the proposed SAS including its components and underlying algorithms. In Sect. 4, the experimental design is explained. Section 5 is the performance evaluation. Finally, the conclusion and future work are presented in Sect. 6.

2 Related Work

This section presents and summarizes the most recent related work that focuses on QoS management processes. Then, it compares this paper with the literature.

QoS is an important concepts in distributed systems such as Grid Computing [16], CC [17], and EC [12]. It covers a wide range of metrics, such as reliability and latency, that represent the SC concerns. In fact, the QoS management in EC environments is not a travel task which can be more complex when considering the SP optimization objectives. Any SP must be aware of the QoS metrics to guarantee the SAL alongside the provider's objectives, such as revenue maximization. These optimization dimensions represent conflicting objectives which can be managed through a SAS.

The management of the QoS in EC via SAS has attracted a lot of attention recently. Its management can be performed on a virtualization level by managing virtual resources. It is also possible to see some other works tackle this issue by managing the incoming workload using scheduling, offloading, and load balancing mechanisms. In this section, the related work will be discussed according to the adaptation level which can be virtualization level (i.e., Virtual Machines (VMs) and containers) or task level.

Virtualization Level: A series of the most recent work focuses on the containerization management in the EC as it is more suitable for EC environments. For instance, an adaptive system architecture is proposed in [18] to adjust the containers reactively in EC with conflicting optimization objectives, which are response time and elasticity, where the response time represent the SC perspective and the elasticity represents the SP perspective. It targets agricultural domain which cannot be neither implemented nor applied on other domains such as smart cities. The proactive adaptation is also can be used to support elasticity of the EC using Neural Network Long Short-Term Memory [19]. The ML models are developed and evaluated using real workload which Taxis in Francisco and Rome. This work is extended in [20] to support QoS in terms of processing time, resource utilization maximization, rejection rate minimization, and system stability. It uses threshold-based mechanism to allow the system acting reactively shaping hybrid SAS.

A thorough research investigation is conducted to compare the reactive and proactive adaptation in CC under different scenarios [21]. It targets the elasticity and taillatency of web applications. The overall results show that the reactive adaptation provide the worst performances as compared to the proactive adaptation approach. Another thorough investigation is conducted targeting the containers migration in Fog Computing (FC) under different migration techniques [22]. The main finding stated that the performance of migration techniques varies according to the network and service conditions.

A limited number of research focuses on the VMs management in the EC. For example, Liu B. et. al., [23] proposes hybrid resource management model using a combination of ML and statistical forecasting models and threshold-based resource utilization.

This work considers a more complex conflicting objectives which are cost constraint, deadline constraints, elasticity, and efficient resource utilization. The proposed model is comprehensively evaluated and compared with other benchmarks which shows its effectiveness. Nonetheless, the use of VM on the EC represents the main weakness as VMs are characterized by high footprint. In [24], task workflow scheduling algorithm for CC is developed with consideration to computational cost and the task deadline. Unlike CC, EC is characterized by, e.g., geo-distributed and limited resources, which need to be considered in scheduling algorithm development.

Task Level: Task level is another common level that can be used to manage the QoS in EC. In [25] a reactive task offloading model is proposed to reduce the energy consumption and delay in Mobile Edge Computing (MEC) environment. The model is developed using NSGA II multi-objective optimization algorithm and energy threshold. Although its evaluation shows its effectiveness, there is some limitation in term of the idle power consumptions that is used by edge devices which needs to be supported by scalability models as well as the lack of energy consumption status of the IoT devices.

Three QoS metrics are considered in [26] which are response time-, energy consumption-, and cost-guarantee. It aims to improve the service discovery and selection using Weighted Acyclic Graph by scheduling the IoT tasks reactively on the IoT layer. In [27], conflicting objectives, which are latency, service time, network usage, and efficient utilization, are managed using location-aware framework. The framework aims to reactively offload the IoT tasks, which are the analysis of multimedia and textual data, to either fog or cloud layers. The results analysis shows that the proposed framework outperforms other benchmarks. The latency is also managed in [4] using reactive architecture. This architecture is designed using agent-based component which is known as broker. It is responsible of scheduling IoT tasks that have several latency requirements ranging from latency sensitive to latency tolerant. The latency-sensitive application in FC-CC environments also attracts the attention of [28]. It proposes a reactive framework for task scheduling on VMs with respect to IoT task priority.

A task management framework for real-time applications in EC is presented in [29]. The framework is designed using two level scheduling, namely, fuzzy logic control system and hierarchical scheduling. The first level of scheduling aims to schedule the tasks on the virtual edge cluster whereas the second level is responsible for determining the task that should be running on the physical processor. The management framework is implemented and evaluated using ExSched where their evaluation requires further analysis and scenarios to prove the effectiveness of such system.

Content delivery application is one of the common applications that utilize EC environment to enhance the QoS in term of contents quality. In [30], a content delivery hybrid architecture that is supported by content delivery mechanism is designed aiming to enhance the video quality and FC resource utilization. The main drawback of this study is the use of statistical analysis prediction method without a clear justification. As compared to statistical methods, ML methods shows a good performance and seen as a future for supporting decision making in EC environments.

A novel MEC reactive framework is presented in [31] to maximize the SP revenue and resource utilization as well as respect the consumer budget. This framework uses task scheduling on the edge layer using Stackelberg Game theory. The MEC layer is assumed to be heterogenous, such as smartphones, tablets, and medium data centers, where the VMs are the provisioned resources. Further, the IoT layer can be consist of, e.g., sensors, smartphones, and PCs, with limited budget. Indeed, the assumption of provision VMs as resources using smartphones and tablets represents the main limitation of such system as these devices have limited resources.

Reliability is another QoS metrics which is targeted by [32]. The authors propose an optimization approach for EC environments using Stochastic Petri Net to consider both edge and cloud layers to support the reliability as a key factor as well as response time. The same metric is also adopted by [33]. A dynamic reliability management technique is proposed targeting the IoT devices with consideration to task deadline and IoT energy consumption. It uses data partition technique to manage the offloaded data size to the edge layer. Although, it targets a sensitive optimization objective, the SP perspective seems ignored as the Edge Nodes (ENs) might be power using renewable energy.

A self-organized decentralized scheme is presented to support EC energy efficiency reactively with consideration to task latency [34]. The proposed mechanism aims to terminate the redundant application instances located in neighbor ENs (i.e., mini-cloud) by consolidating the workload.

Related Work Summary: AS compared to the presented papers, this research develops a novel SAS for EC environment that consists of elasticity- and QoS-framework. Further, a comprehensive investigates is conducted in our previous work [14] to compare the performance of proactive, reactive, and hybrid adaptation in EC environments under different scenarios. The elasticity framework is designed and evaluated in our previous work [14, 15]. The QoS framework, which is the main contribution of this paper, extends the previous work by proposing a framework with its underlying algorithms that considers conflicting objective. These objectives are *acceptance rate maximization*, which represents the SP perspective, and *processing time minimization*, whereby it is the consumer concerns. Moreover, the QoS framework is designed according to simulation-based comprehensive investigation to select the most suitable task scheduling algorithm, proper resource utilization threshold, and proper resource monitoring interval. Moreover, the proposed SAS has the ability to manage two levels which are virtualization and task levels whereas, to the best of our knowledge, the exist work targets either virtualized or task level. A summary of the presented work as compared to our work is presented in Table 1 based on the essential SAS requirements, that must be addressed, which can be captured using the 5W and 1H questions [35, 36]: *When to adapt? Why do we have to adapt? Where do we have to implement change? What kind of change is needed? Who has to perform the adaptation? How is the adaptation performed?* In this paper, the Who question is ignored as the user/system administrator is not involved in the adaptation process, which is also ignored by [36].

3 System Architecture

This work extends our previous works [13–15] by including the QoS framework as part of the SAS architecture that is presented in Fig. 1, where the main contribution of this paper is highlighted in grey. The framework components and the underlying algorithms are presented in the following sections focusing on the QoS components only whereas other components description can be found in [14, 15].

Table 1. Related work comparison.

Paper	Layers	Adaptation questions				
		Where	When	Why	What	How
[18]	Edge	Containers	Reactive	Elasticity Response time	Number of provisioned resources	Instantiate/terminate containers
[19] [20]	Edge	Containers	Hybrid	Elasticity Resources utilization Processing time Stability	Location of processing task Number of provisioned resources	Instantiate/terminate containers Offloading
[21]	Cloud	Containers	Proactive Reactive	Elasticity Latency	Number of provisioned resources	Instantiate/terminate VMs
[22]	Edge	Containers	Reactive	-	Location of containers	Migration
[23]	Edge	VMs	Hybrid	Elasticity Cost Deadline Resource utilization	Location of processing task Number of provisioned resources	Instantiate/terminate VMs Load balancing
[24]	Cloud	VMs	Reactive	Cost Deadline	Location of processing task	Scheduling
[25]	IoT-Edge	Tasks	Reactive	Energy Delay	Location of processing task	Offloading
[26]	IoT	Tasks	Reactive	Response time Energy Cost	Location of processing task	Scheduling

(continued)

Table 1. (*continued*)

Paper	Layers	Adaptation questions				
		Where	When	Why	What	How
[27]	Edge-Cloud	Tasks	Reactive	Latency Service time Resource utilization Network usage	Location of processing task	Offloading Load balancing
[4]	Edge	Tasks	Reactive	Latency	Location of processing task	Scheduling
[28]	Edge-Cloud	Tasks	Reactive	Latency	Location of processing task	Scheduling
[29]	Edge	Tasks	Reactive	Deadline	Location of processing task	Scheduling
[30]	Edge	Tasks	Hybrid	Content quality Resource utilization	Location of the contents	EN selection
[31]	Edge	Tasks	Reactive	Revenue Cost Resources utilization	Location of processing task	Scheduling
[32]	Edge-Cloud	Tasks	Reactive	Reliability	Location of processing task	Scheduling
[33]	IoT-Edge	Tasks	Reactive	Reliability Deadline Bandwidth Energy	Location of processing task Amount of transferred data	Offloading Data partitioning
[34]	Edge	–	–	Energy	Number of application instances	Decreases the number of application instances
This paper	Edge-Cloud	Containers Tasks	Hybrid	Elasticity Processing time Acceptance rate Resource utilization	Number of provisioned resources Location of processing task	Instantiate/terminate containers Scheduling

3.1 Proposed QoS Framework

The Monitor, Analyze, Plan, and Execute (MAPE)-based control loop is adopted in designing the proposed QoS framework. The adaptation activities enable the SAS to manage and control the lifecycle of the running resources/application in the operational environment. These activities play an essential role to guarantee the QoS level with consideration to the SP objectives thanks to the full MAPE loop. This means the QoS framework must be designed to cover these activities. Hence, the proposed framework includes several components which can be allocated to each MAPE activity, as shown in Fig. 1.

- **Monitor:** It collects the run-time raw data from the operational infrastructure, such as the number of running containers and Central Processing Unit (CPU) utilization, according to the specified time interval (see Sect. 4.1). The collected data will be stored in the Resource Utilization Repository (RU-Repository) which is the main QoS component in the monitor activity. The RU-Repository was only considering the number of running containers in the elasticity framework version. In this paper, the RU-repository is extended to collect the CPU utilization of the ENs as it is an important parameter in the QoS management process to avoid resource overutilization which degrade the application performance and cause high delay.
- **Analyze:** It analyzes the collected data by the monitor component. The analysis involves running containers and calculating average CPU utilization which are the main parameters in the adaptive process. The analysis process is conducted by the Resource Utilization Analyzer (RU-Analyzer) which is further explained in Sect. 3.2. The RU-Analyzer is extended in this paper to consider the CPU utilization of the ENs as the CPU threshold is an essential parameter to guarantee the QoS.
- **Plan:** It takes the acceptance/rejection decisions based on the analysis outcomes that are provided by the analysis activity where the QoS decisions are made by QoS manager component.
- **Execute:** It includes the admission control component which is responsible for accepting/rejecting the tasks on arrival according to the decisions that are made by the QoS manager. The admission control is also responsible for ensuring the consistency between both elasticity framework decisions and QoS framework decisions.

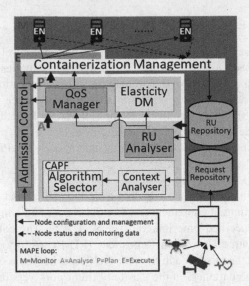

Fig. 1. Proposed self-adaptive system [14].

Table 2. Notations.

Symbol	Definition
CPU_j^{Uti}	CPU utilization for an edge node
CPU_{stat}	CPU utilization status
CPU_{thr}	CPU utilization threshold
CPU_{avg}	Average CPU utilization for the edge cluster
$Cont_{SB}^{a_x}$	# of stand-by containers for requested application
QoS_{dec}	QoS algorithm decision

Algorithm 1. QoS manager.

Input: CPU_j^{Uti} and CPU_{thr}

Output: CPU_{stat} and QoS_{dec}

```
0:  Begin
1:  For each time interval do
2:      Calculate  CPU_avg ← (Σ_{j=1}^{n} CPU_j^{uti}) / n
3:      If (CPU_avg < CPU^{thr})
4:          CPU_stat ← Underuitlization
5:          QoS_dec ← Accept
6:      Else
7:          CPU_stat ← Overutilization
8:          QoS_dec ← Reject
9:      End if
10: End for
11: End
```

3.2 Algorithms

The proposed QoS framework is supported by two algorithms, namely, QoS manager and admission control.

QoS Manager Algorithm: Its pseudocode is presented in Algorithm 1 where the notations are listed in Table 2. This algorithm relies on a threshold-based resource utilization mechanism where the suitable threshold will be determined experimentally. It aims to identify the resource utilization status; thus, the acceptance/ rejection decision can be made. For each time interval, it starts by calculating the average CPU utilization (line 1 and 2) where the monitoring time interval of collecting the resource usage will be determined experimentally. It then compares the average CPU utilization with the CPU utilization threshold (line 3). If the average utilization is below the specified threshold, it updates both resource utilization status and QoS decision by underutilization and accept, respectively (line 4 and 5). Otherwise, the resource utilization status and QoS decision will be updated to overutilization and reject, respectively (line 6–8).

Admission Control Algorithm: Its pseudocode is presented in Algorithm 2. It aims to accept/reject the incoming IoT requests according to both resource utilization status, which is determined by the QoS manager algorithm, and the number of stand-by containers that are instantiated by the elasticity framework. Firstly, it checks the resource utilization status (line 2). If its status equals to overutilization, then, it rejects the incoming tasks during the current time interval (line 3). Otherwise, it checks the availability of number of stand-by containers which has the same request type (line 5). If there is any container ready to accommodate the incoming requests, the requests will be accepted (line 6). If not, the request will be rejected (line 7 and 8).

Algorithm 2. Admission control.
Input: $Cont_{SB}^{a_x}$ and CPU_{stat}
Output: Adaptive decision (i.e., acceptance/ rejection) of the request
0: **Begin**
1: **While** true **do**
2:      **If** ($CPU_{stat} ==$ Overutilization)
3:          **Reject** request
4:      **Else**
5:          **If** ($Cont_{SB}^{a_x} > 0$)
6:              **Accept** request
7:          **Else**
8:              **Reject** request
9:          **End if**
10:     **End if**
11: **End while**
12: **End**

4   Experimental Design

In this section, the experimental design is presented. It includes the experiments' objective and scenario, workload dataset, evaluation metrics, and experimental settings.

4.1   Experiments' Objective and Scenario

In this paper, as stated in Sect. 1, the aim is to develop a QoS framework that is able to satisfy both SP objective, in term of *acceptance rate maximization*, and SC, in term of *latency*. In EC, latency might be related to, e.g., network or processing delay, where this paper focuses on the processing time delay which can be minimized by avoiding overutilization of the resources. To do so, the scheduling algorithm, CPU utilization threshold, and resource monitoring interval must be investigated and evaluated according to the operational environment.

Therefore, five different task scheduling algorithms will be evaluated with different CPU threshold and resource monitoring intervals under different workloads. The targeted algorithms are *random-fit*, *worst-fit*, *best-fit*, *first-fit*, and *next-fit*, where these algorithms are common and well-known benchmark algorithms. Further, the considered CPU utilization thresholds and resource monitoring intervals are *70%, 75%, 80%, 85%, 90%*, and *95%*, and 1 s, 5 s, 10 s, and 15 s, respectively. A summary of the experimental settings is provided in Table 3.

4.2 Workload Dataset

This paper uses the Shanghai Telecom dataset [37], which has six-month historical record for mobile phones accessing the internet services. These mobile phones are connected to base stations which are distributed over Shanghai city. It is a well-known dataset that are used previously by, e.g. [38–40].

To be more specific, the same workload patterns (i.e., decreasing, increasing, and fluctuating) will be considered as in our previous work [14]. However, these patterns show a limited CPU utilization. Therefore, in this work, the synthetic workload is generated by multiplying the original workload by 10, 20, and 30. For instance, if the first minute in the original dataset has 10 requests, the new datasets will have 100, 200, and 300 requests. This helps evaluating the proposed framework and the underlying algorithm under different and higher workloads. So, we will have three datasets, namely, X10, X20, and X30 where each dataset has the mentioned workload patterns, i.e., decreasing, increasing, and fluctuating. A summary of the datasets can be found in Table 3.

4.3 Evaluation Metrics

Three performance metrics are used which are *average acceptance rate*, *average CPU utilization*, and *average processing time*. The selection of both acceptance rate and CPU utilization is important to evaluate the proposed framework from the SP perspective. In the other hand, the processing time is used to evaluate the framework from the SC perspective.

4.4 Simulation Setting

A simulation-based experiments are conducted using EdgeCloudSim [41] to evaluate the proposed framework and the underlying algorithms. It provides an environment specific to edge computing scenarios, and is built on the CloudSim simulator. It has the ability to simulate the IoT environments including both edge and cloud layers with possibility to customize the scenario by considering single-tier, two-tier, and two-tier with edge-orchestrator. In this paper, we only consider the IoT and edge layers. The environment is simulated for 14 min duration time, where the first minute for the warm-up period, and the last minute to allow releasing the resources and completing the jobs. The edge layer is assumed to have single a cluster with four ENs, each node with four cores and 2000 Million Instructions Per Second as processing speed. Moreover, the simulation will be conducted using mixed applications where each application brings different computational requirements. These applications are Face Recognition (FC), Emergency Traffic Management (ETM), Augmented Reality (AR), Health Monitoring (HM), Industrial Health Monitoring (IHM), and Intelligent Parking (IP). The most important simulation parameters are listed in Table 3 where the rest can be found in [14] including the system model and assumptions.

Table 3. Simulation settings.

Parameter	Value
Scheduling algorithms	Random fit, Worst fit, Best fit, First fit, and Next fit
CPU utilization threshold (%)	70, 75, 80, 85, 90, and 95
Resource status update interval (Sec.)	1, 5, 10, and 15
Workload datasets	Decreasing (X10, X20, X30), Increasing (X10, X20, X30), and Fluctuating (X10, X20, X30)
Provided applications	6 (FR, ETM, AR, HM, IHM, and IP)
# of requests (Decreasing: X10, X20, X30 / Increasing: X10, X20, X30 / Fluctuating: X10, X20, X30)	(Decreasing: 1150, 2300, 3450 / Increasing: 3310, 6620, 9930 / Fluctuating: 3340, 6680, 10020)

5 Performance Evaluation

This section, firstly, presents the experimental results by headlighting the impact of the targeted parameters, i.e., scheduling algorithms, resource utilization threshold, and resource monitoring interval, according to the framework objectives. It then discusses the presented results emphasizing on the overall performance and metrics and workload relationships. Additionally, it presents the most suitable values of each parameter that optimizes the objectives that can be used in the proposed QoS framework. Finally, it highlights the main findings and proposes recommendations accordingly.

5.1 Objectives' Evaluation

In this section the performance of the scheduling algorithms will be categorized into two categories, which are category (A), which includes next- and random-fit, and category (B), which includes best-, first-, and worst-fit. This categorization is important to facilitate the discussion. Note that each algorithm in the same category provides almost the same results. Next, the configuration notation (95,1) means 95% resource threshold and 1 s monitoring interval.

Acceptance Rate Maximization
Scheduling Algorithm Impact: The results of the scheduling algorithms show a significant variation in the acceptance rate over the considered datasets. This variation becomes observable as the workload increases as presented in Fig. 2. However, for the lowest workload (i.e., X10-decreasing pattern), the acceptance rate is almost the same, which is between 98.3%–90.67% overall scheduling algorithms. Further, this difference increases as the workload increase where the performance of category (A)- and category (B) algorithms can be observed. For instance, if the best-fit is compared with random-fit using X10-, X20-, and X30-fluctuating pattern as shown in Fig. 2. It can be seen that the random-fit outperforms the best-fit overall configurations and datasets. Considering Fig. 2A and 2B, in one hand, the worst performance is provided by best-fit under

(70,15) configuration, which equals to 73.91%, whereas the best performance equals to 88.63 under (95,1) configuration. On the other hand, the worst acceptance rate of the random-fit is 87.49% when the configuration is (70, 10) whereas the best performance is provided under configuration (95,1) which equals to 89.98. This difference increases as the workload increases as seen in Figs. 2C, 2D, 2E, and 2F.

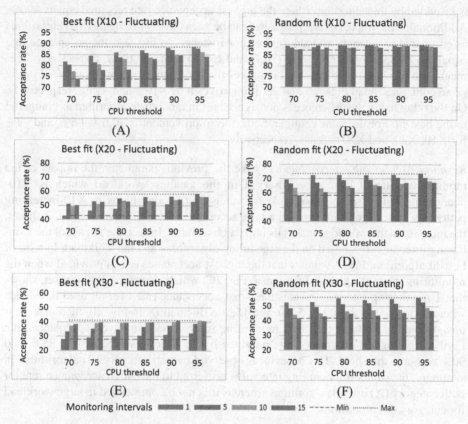

Fig. 2. Acceptance rate comparison.

For example, in X30 workload, if the highest acceptance rate provided by best-fit is compared with the highest acceptance rate provided by random-fit algorithm. The results indicate that random-fit can provide up to 35% better performance which is a significant improvement in the acceptance rate. In conclusion, the results show that the selection of the most suitable scheduling algorithm plays a major role to improve the acceptance rate.

Resource Utilization Threshold Impact: The resource utilization threshold has also an impact on the acceptance rate. This impact can be observed when the workload increases. Like the scheduling algorithm, its impact cannot be seen in X10-decreasing pattern. In Fig. 2A, it can be clearly seen that the increase in the threshold contributes to maximizing the acceptance rate for best-fit. In the other hand, its impact cannot be seen in Fig. 2B which shows the acceptance rate for the random-fit due to the great performance that is provided by this algorithm where the highest acceptance rate recorded equals ~90%. Additionally, the impact of this parameter can be seen clearly in category (B) algorithms as compared to category (A) algorithms. For instance, in Fig. 2A, the acceptance rate equals to 81.83% and 87.82% for (70,1) and (95,1) configurations, respectively. This means the increase in the threshold improves the acceptance rate by about 6%. For the same configuration in Figs. 2C and 2E, it improves it by ~19% and ~15%, respectively. On the other hand, the difference is not significant in random-fit algorithm as compared to the best-fit. For the same configurations, the improvement is ~0.6%, ~6%, and ~7% for X10, X20, and X30 datasets, respectively.

Resource Monitoring Interval Impact: Like the previous parameter, the impact of the monitoring interval cannot be observed in the smallest workload which is X10-decreasing. It is also not observable for category (A) algorithms in X10-increasing pattern as these algorithms provide a high acceptance rate. However, as Fig. 2 shows, the increase in the workload makes its impact observable. In fact, the impact of the monitoring interval varies based on the scheduling algorithms and the workload. In term of best-fit algorithm, Fig. 2A shows that the highest acceptance rate is provided when the monitoring interval equals 1. In contrast, Fig. 2C, which shows the X20 dataset, shows that 1 monitoring interval provides the worst acceptance rate over all used thresholds whereas the other values, i.e., 5, 10, and 15, are fluctuating. In Fig. 2E, there is a clear upward pattern showing that the 1 monitoring interval has the lowest acceptance rate. Further, the highest acceptance rate provided by 15 over 70%, 75%, 80%, 85%, and 90% resource threshold. This behavior is observed overall category (B) algorithms. In summary, the smallest monitoring interval is preferred to have high acceptance rate for both category (A) and (B) algorithms whereas it is not recommended in large workload for category (B) algorithms.

Processing Time Minimization

Scheduling Algorithm Impact: scheduling algorithms have a significant impact on the processing time. This impact can be seen clearly even when the workload is very low. Figure 2 compares the processing time that obtained by best-fit, i.e., left column, and random-fit, i.e., right column, under X10, X20, and X30 datasets for the fluctuating pattern. The difference can be clearly seen over all configurations. For instance, if the longest processing time provided by random-fit is compared with the shortest processing time provided by the best-fit, it can be found that the processing time provided by the best-fit is almost the double processing time provided by random-fit. In other words, the longest processing time provided by random-fit equals 1.39 s. under (95,15) configuration for X10 dataset whereas the shortest processing time almost more than the double of this value, which is provided by (85,15) configuration. This finding can be generalized to all algorithms in both categories. The impact of the scheduling algorithm on the processing time is not limited to reducing the processing time but it also helps maintaining the increase of the processing time when the workload increases. Figure 4 presets the processing time for all algorithms under (95,1) configuration. It is clear that category (B) algorithms experience faster growth than category (A).

Resource Utilization Threshold Impact: The impact of the resource utilization threshold is limited across all algorithms and workloads. It does not show any impact on the X10 datasets across all workload's patterns. For the X20 dataset, its impact can be seen in increasing and fluctuating patterns for next- and random-fit where the increase in the threshold increases the processing time. Figure 3 depicts its impact on the fluctuating pattern. Generally, its impact follows some form of randomness across the datasets, but it is observable when the interval equals to 1 s. in X20 random-fit as shown in Fig. 3D, and X30 for best- and random-fit as shown in Fig. 3E and 3F, respectively. It also appears in the X30-decreasing pattern for both best- and next-fit algorithms when the monitoring interval equals to 15 and 1, respectively. To conclude, its impact is related to the scheduling algorithm, resource monitoring interval, and adopted workload.

Resource Monitoring Interval Impact: Similar to the threshold impact, generally, the monitoring interval does not have any impact on the X10 datasets as the processing time shows some form of randomness. However, its impact can be seen in X20 datasets for increasing and fluctuating patterns on next- and random-fit, as shown in Fig. 5, where it is clear in the next-fit as shown in Fig. 5A and 5C. In case of random-fit, its impact is limited and constraint by the resource threshold values (i.e., 75% and 80%). The results show that the increase in the monitoring interval increases the processing time which causes high delay. In contrast, the best-fit algorithm under fluctuating workload shows that a smaller monitoring interval leads to higher processing time.

In the X30 dataset, next-fit overall patterns provide the same results where the increase in the monitoring interval increases the processing time. This finding is also provided by random-fit under decreasing pattern. The same impact can slightly be observed when random-fit is used in both X30-increasing and -fluctuating patterns for the small resource threshold values (i.e., 70%, 75%, and 80%) where its impact is reversed for the large threshold. For the best- and first-fit in X30 datasets, the smallest monitoring interval, i.e., 1 s, provides highest processing time in decreasing and fluctuating patterns where other values show some discrepancy. For the increasing pattern, it shows roughly the opposite.

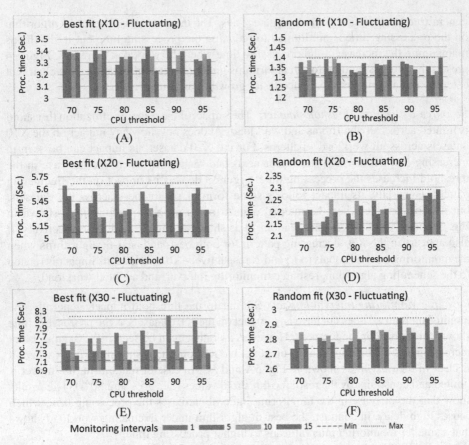

Fig. 3. Processing time comparison.

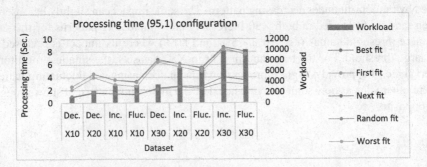

Fig. 4. Impact of workload on the processing time.

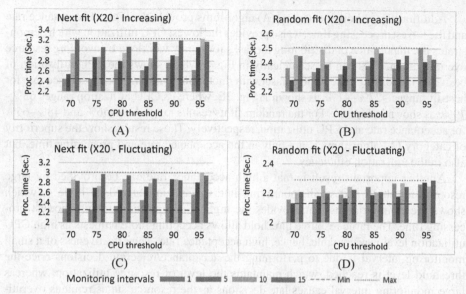

Fig. 5. Processing time.

5.2 Results Discussion

The results will be discussed based on the *overall performance* of the algorithms, threshold, and monitoring interval and the *relationship analysis* among the adopted metrics and workloads.

Overall Performance: As presented in the previous section, in pursuance of providing high acceptance rate and low processing time, category (A) algorithms are experience an extremely great performance as compared to other algorithms.In fact, a possible explanation for the great performance provided by these algorithms can be their ability to provide efficient scheduling. These algorithms schedule each request on different nodes and avoid resource overutilization as the workload experiences burstiness. For instance, next-fit is able to distribute the incoming tasks due to the use of scheduling pointer which schedule a new task in the next suitable EN. Suppose that two tasks came at the same time, the next-fit will schedule the first task on the first suitable EN where the second task will be scheduled in the next suitable EN. In case of first-fit, it will schedule both tasks on the first suitable EN, hence, resource overutilization, long processing time and high rejection rate. This case is also applicable to other algorithms from the same category (i.e., category (B)).

Further, the systematic behavior of next-fit algorithm, in scheduling the tasks, explains the clear patterns that are shown in its results where the effect of both resource threshold and monitoring interval are clear as compared to other algorithms. On the other hand, random-fit algorithm will distribute these tasks randomly across the nodes, which shows some lack of consistency in some results.

Additionally, although category (A) algorithms provide the highest acceptance rate and the lowest processing time, it also provides the lowest CPU utilization which demonstrates the importance of distributing the tasks for bursty workload by avoiding resource overutilization. This can be seen clearly in Fig. 6 which shows the CPU utilization of best- and random-fit under X30 dataset with fluctuating pattern. The acceptance rate for best-fit ranges ~27%–41%, as shown in Fig. 2E, where its CPU utilization ranges 63%–79%, as shown in Fig. 6A. For the random-fit its results range 41%–56% and 48%–65% for acceptance rate and CPU utilization, respectively. These results show the superiority of category (A) algorithms is not only in the acceptance rate and processing time, but also in the utilization efficiency.

Another important result is that a high acceptance rate can be provided by large resource threshold and small monitoring interval as summarized in Table 4, which shows the configurations that provides the highest acceptance rate and shortest processing time. The large resource threshold allows accepting more requests as high CPU utilization level is acceptable, hence, high acceptance rate. The effectiveness of a small monitoring interval is due to performing the acceptance/rejection decisions once the threshold level is reached, which maintains the level of resource utilization, whereas large monitoring interval causes late decisions as the resource status remains overutilization for long period. In contrast, the shortest processing time can be provided with small resource threshold and roughly small resource monitoring interval. In this case, a small resource threshold reduces the overhead on the EN resources by rejecting some workload early when the CPU utilization level is low, thus, short processing time. Similar to the acceptance rate case, a small monitoring interval allows updating the resource status immediately once the threshold condition is satisfied whereas large monitoring interval causes late updates.

Table 4. The most efficient configurations.

Dataset		Maximum acceptance rate provided by:				Minimum processing time provided by:			
		Value	Algorithm	CPU threshold	Monitoring interval	Value	Algorithm	CPU threshold	Monitoring interval
X10	Dec.	90.67	Worst	85	1	0.84	Next	70	15
	Inc.	92.67	Next	95	10	1.28	Next	75	1
	Fluc.	91.63	Next	90	1	1.19	Next	75	5
X20	Dec.	89.19	Next	85	5	1.5	Next	85	1
	Inc.	76.17	Next	95	1	2.28	Random	70	5
	Fluc.	77.29	Next	95	1	2.13	Random	70	5
X30	Dec.	83.21	Next	95	1	2.11	Random	80	5
	Inc.	55.55	Random	90	1	2.95	Random	70	5
	Fluc.	55.96	Random	95	1	2.73	Random	70	1

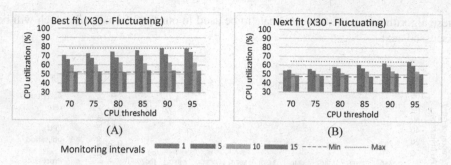

Fig. 6. CPU utilization comparison

Relationship Analysis: It examines the relationship among the evaluation metrics as well as the adopted workload. Not only this but it also evaluates the possibility of generalizing the proposed framework by using different applications and workload pattern. Thus, some of the relationships will be presented in this section using random-fit under (95,1) configuration.

As Fig. 7 depicts, there is an inverse relationship between the acceptance rate and other parameters (i.e., CPU utilization, processing time, and workload) where the acceptance rate decreases as the other parameters increases. This is because of the limited resources located at the edge layer. This can be proved by analyzing the reasons behind task failure in our infrastructure is analyzed for increasing pattern over X10, X20, and X30 datasets, as shown in Fig. 8A, 8B, and 8C, respectively. Mainly, tasks are failed due to elasticity framework as presented in Fig. 8A, where random-fit possibly failed in scheduling some tasks on the ENs due to it random selection. The elasticity percentage decreases as the workload increases in X20 and X30 dataset where CPU threshold shows the highest reason behind the failures due to the CPU utilization that experienced in the high workload. This also explains the reason behind the downward trend in the acceptance rate which means that the received workload starts exceeding the infrastructure capacity where the maximum acceptance rate can be provided ~92%.

It also shows that there is a close relationship between the CPU utilization, processing time, and workload where both CPU utilization and processing time increase as the workload increases. This is expected as more workload is submitted to the ENs which causes high resource utilization, hence, high processing time.

5.3 Framework Design

Indeed, the design of the QoS framework with consideration to three parameters, which are scheduling algorithm, resource threshold, and monitoring interval, is not a trivial task due to the consideration of the conflicting objectives to fulfill. As presented in the previous sections, the scheduling algorithms have a significant impact on both objectives (i.e., acceptance rate maximization and processing time minimization). It was shown that the category (A) algorithms provide the highest acceptance rate and lowest processing time where their performance can be also affected by the resource threshold and monitoring interval. Further, these algorithms provide roughly the same performance. Thus, these algorithms are the best candidate to be used in our QoS framework which will be discussed next.

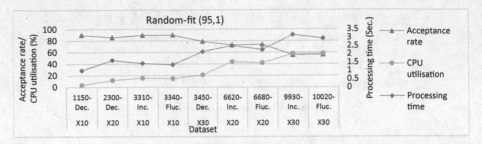

Fig. 7. Evaluation metrics and workload relashionship

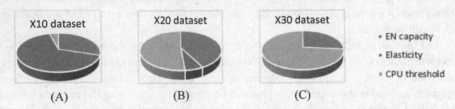

Fig. 8. Failed reason – increasing pattern.

However, the consideration of both threshold and monitoring interval remains a challenge. The results show that higher acceptance rate is provided by large threshold and small monitoring interval whereas the shortest processing time is provided by small threshold and small monitoring interval in the most cases. Thus, the results that are provided by both algorithms over different resource threshold and 1 s. monitoring interval need further analysis to find a borderline that satisfies both objectives. The selection of 1 s. as the most proper monitoring interval is because it provides the highest acceptance rate and lowest processing time in most cases. This, however, is derived experimentally.

The threshold effect for both algorithms is analyzed as presented in Fig. 9A and 9B by emphasizing on 95% colored in orang triangle and 70% colored in blue square as these values represent the highest and lowest acceptance rate. Figure 9A shows that the difference in the acceptance rate in the X10 dataset is not significant where it becomes significant in X20 and X30 dataset. The improvement can up to ~6% in some cases by 95% threshold, e.g., X20 increasing and fluctuating patterns, if the largest threshold, i.e., 95%, is compared with the smallest threshold, i.e., 70%. The same finding is also can be seen in random-fit algorithm as presented in Fig. 9B.

In Fig. 10, the processing time for the same algorithms are compared. Both figures, i.e., 10A and 10B, show almost the same finding as in Fig. 9. However, in Fig. 10A the difference between the threshold results provided by 95% and 70% can reach ~21% where the difference seems to increase as the workload increases. In Fig. 9B, this difference is very low, which can reach ~6%.

From the above discussion, there is a trade-off between the acceptance rate maximization and processing time minimization. Generally, it seems that 95% is the best candidate to be used in our framework. However, doing further comparison is important to take the final decision by comparing the 95% threshold results of category (A) algorithms as it provides the highest acceptance rate, the best results provided overall experiments, 70% threshold from next-fit algorithm as it seems that borderline between the acceptance rate and processing time.

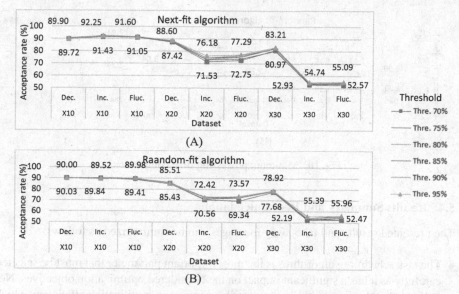

Fig. 9. Maximum acceptance rate comparison.

Figure 11A and 11B show the highest acceptance rate overall experiments as compared to next-fit (95/70,1) and random fit (95,1) and shortest processing time overall experiment as compared to next-fit (95/70,1) and random-fit (95,1), respectively. From Fig. 11A, it is clear that next- fit (95,1) provides either the highest acceptance rate in most cases or the closest configuration to the highest acceptance rate (i.e., shaded in green). In contrast, it provides the worst processing time as shown in Fig. 11B. If both next-fit (70,1) and random-fit (95,1) are compared, it is clear that both provide roughly the same results where the next-fit provides higher acceptance rate in most cases and roughly lower processing time in most cases too. If these configurations are compared with the configurations that provide the highest acceptance rate and lowest processing time, it can be observed that they provide acceptable acceptance rate and very close processing time to the lowest values. Thus, it can be stated that although the next-fit (95,1) provides the highest acceptance rate, it cannot be used as it provides long processing time. In term of random-fit (95,1), it is a good candidate, but it seems that next (70,1) is the best candidate, even when it has small resource threshold, as to shows a great performance to consider both objectives.

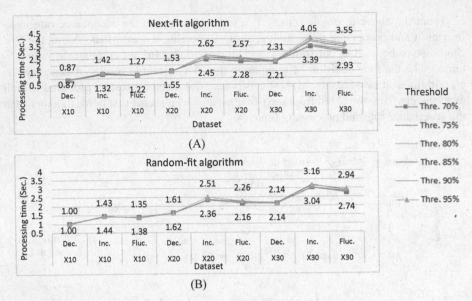

Fig. 10. Minimum processing time comparison.

5.4 Results Summary and Recommendations

The presented results and take-away messages can be summarized as follows:

- The task scheduling algorithms is the most important parameter that must be selected carefully as it has a significant impact on the considered optimization objectives. Not only this but these algorithms can contribute to resource utilization efficiency, which helps maximizing the acceptance rate and maintaining the processing time.
- The selection of scheduling algorithm must be performed with consideration to workload pattern and users' behavior as it might affect the overall performance.
- The resource threshold has a significant impact on the acceptance rate while in the processing time it is in relation to scheduling algorithms and the monitoring interval parameter.
- The resource monitoring interval effect can be seen clearly on the acceptance rate. However, its effect is related to the adopted scheduling algorithm and workload pattern for processing time. Further, for category (A) algorithms, increasing the monitoring interval negatively affects the acceptance rate. In contrast, it improves the acceptance rate for category (B) algorithms.
- It is an essential step to evaluate the EC infrastructure including the key parameters, such as scheduling algorithms, resource threshold, and monitoring interval, as these parameters might significantly improve/reduce the infrastructure performance. Moreover, this step becomes more important in case of considering conflicting objectives where the trad-offs always exist.
- Making the SAS aware of the operational environment can be core to improve the system performance. This becomes essential in EC SAS as the IoT characterized by its workload dynamicity and fluctuating as some of adopted configurations might be

suitable for small or specific workload pattern. Indeed, as results show, some of these SAS configurations show great performance for small workload but once the workload becomes extremely high another configuration becomes preferable.

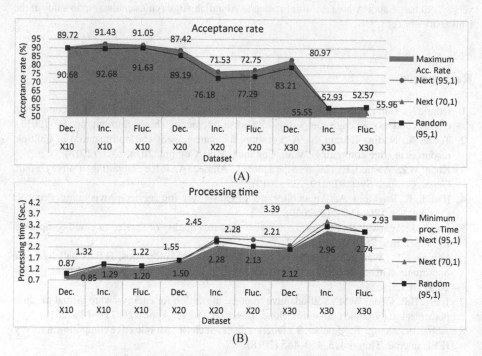

Fig. 11. The best results overall experiments comparison.

6   Conclusion and Future Work

QoS management process is a complex process due to the nature of both EC environment and IoT devices. Its complexity increases when SP's concerns are considered. Thus, this paper has presented a novel QoS framework to support conflicting objectives, i.e., service provided and SC. The proposed framework is embedded in a SAS that targets both elasticity and QoS problems. This framework is supported by two algorithms, namely, QoS manager and admission control. Further, the proposed framework is evaluated extensively under several configurations that are related to task scheduling algorithms, where five algorithms are examined, resource utilization threshold and monitoring interval period. The results reveal that the considered parameters have a significant impact on the optimization objectives, which can be e.g., up-to ~35% and more than half for acceptance rate and processing time, respectively. As future work, the proposed SAS can be extended to consider the CC layer for offloading process based on pre-defied policies. Further, these policies are expected to consider the IoT application requirements and profiles, such as application priority and both computational and communicational requirements. This is expected to improve both acceptance rate and avoid SLA violation, thus, maximize the SP's revenue.

Acknowledgement. The authors would like to acknowledge Prince Sattam bin Abdulaziz University, Alkharj, Saudi Arabia, for full funding to Abdullah Aljulayfi's scholarship to study at the University of Leeds, UK.

References

1. Dolui, K., Datta, S.K.: Comparison of edge computing implementations: fog computing, cloudlet and mobile edge computing. In: Global Internet of Things Summit, pp. 1–6 (2017)
2. Toczé, K., Nadjm-Tehrani, S.: A taxonomy for management and optimization of multiple resources in edge computing. Wirel. Commun. Mob. Comput. **2018**, 1–20 (2018)
3. Khan, W.Z., Ahmed, E., Hakak, S., Yaqoob, I., Ahmed, A.: Edge computing: a survey. Futur. Gener. Comput. Syst. **97**, 219–235 (2019)
4. Badidi, E., Ragmani, A.: An architecture for QoS-aware fog service provisioning. Procedia Comput. Sci. **170**, 411–418 (2020)
5. Singh, J., Agarwal, S., Mishra, J.: A review: towards quality of service in cloud computing. Int. J. Sci. Res. **78**, 555–561 (2017)
6. Varghese, B., Wang, N., Barbhuiya, S., Kilpatrick, P., Nikolopoulos, D.S.: Challenges and opportunities in edge computing. In: IEEE International Conference on Smart Cloud, pp. 20–26. IEEE (2016)
7. Jiang, H.P., Chen, W.M.: Self-adaptive resource allocation for energy-aware virtual machine placement in dynamic computing cloud. J. Netw. Comput. Appl. **120**, 119–129 (2018)
8. Abbas, N., Zhang, Y., Member, S., Taherkordi, A., Skeie, T.: Mobile edge computing: a survey. IEEE Internet Things J. **5**, 450–465 (2018)
9. Bahreini, T., Badri, H., Grosu, D.: An envy-free auction mechanism for resource allocation in edge computing systems. In: The 3rd IEEE/ACM Symposium on Edge Computing, pp. 313–322. IEEE (2018)
10. Fan, Q., Ansari, N., Sun, X.: Energy driven avatar migration in green cloudlet networks. IEEE Commun. Lett. **21**, 1601–1604 (2017)
11. Vailshery, L.S.: Internet of Things (IoT) and non-IoT active device connections worldwide from 2010 to 2025. https://www.statista.com/statistics/1101442/iot-number-of-connected-devices-worldwide/. Accessed 29 Nov 2021
12. Taherizadeh, S., Jones, A.C., Taylor, I., Zhao, Z., Stankovski, V.: Monitoring self-adaptive applications within edge computing frameworks: a state-of-the-art review. J. Syst. Softw. **136**, 19–38 (2018). https://doi.org/10.1016/j.jss.2017.10.033
13. Aljulayfi, A.F., Djemame, K.: A novel QoS and energy-aware self-adaptive system architecture for efficient resource management in an edge computing environment. In: The 35th Annual UK Performance Engineering Workshop, pp. 39–54 (2019)
14. Aljulayfi, A.F., Djemame, K.: Towards elastic edge computing environments : an investigation of adaptive approaches. In: The 17th International Conference on Autonomic and Autonomous Systems, pp. 1–10 (2021)
15. Aljulayfi, A.F., Djemame, K.: A machine learning based context-aware prediction framework for edge computing environments. In: The 11th International Conference on Cloud Computing and Services Science, pp. 143–150 (2021)

16. Truong, H.L., Samborski, R., Fahringer, T.: Towards a framework for monitoring and analyzing QoS metrics of grid services. In: The 2nd IEEE International Conference on e-Science and Grid Computing, pp. 1–8 (2006)

17. Ardagna, D., Casale, G., Ciavotta, M., Pérez, J.F., Wang, W.: Quality-of-service in cloud computing: modeling techniques and their applications. J. Internet Serv. Appl. **5**(1), 1–17 (2014). https://doi.org/10.1186/s13174-014-0011-3

18. Nadig, D., El Alaoui, S., Ramamurthy, B., Pitla, S.: ERGO: A scalable edge computing architecture for infrastructureless agricultural internet of things. In: IEEE International Symposium on Local and Metropolitan Area Networks, pp. 1–2. IEEE (2021)

19. Nguyen, C., Klein, C., Elmroth, E.: Multivariate LSTM-based location-aware workload prediction for edge data centers. In: The 19th IEEE/ACM International Symposium on Cluster, Cloud and Grid Computing, pp. 341–350. IEEE (2019)

20. Nguyen, C., Klein, C., Elmroth, E.: Elasticity control for latency-intolerant mobile edge applications. In: The 5th ACM/IEEE Symposium on Edge Computing, pp. 70–83 (2020)

21. Aslanpour, M.S., Toosi, A.N., Gaire, R., Cheema, M.A.: Auto-scaling of web applications in clouds: a tail latency evaluation. In: The 13th IEEE/ACM International Conference on Utility and Cloud Computing, pp. 186–195 (2020)

22. Puliafito, C., Vallati, C., Mingozzi, E., Merlino, G., Longo, F., Puliafito, A.: Container migration in the fog: a performance evaluation. Sensors **19**, 1–22 (2019)

23. Liu, B., Guo, J., Li, C., Luo, Y.: Workload forecasting based elastic resource management in edge cloud. Comput. Ind. Eng. **139**, 1–12 (2020)

24. Arabnejad, V., Bubendorfer, K., Ng, B.: Scheduling deadline constrained scientific workflows on dynamically provisioned cloud resources. Futur. Gener. Comput. Syst. **75**, 348–364 (2017). https://doi.org/10.1016/j.future.2017.01.002

25. Abbasi, M., Mohammadi-Pasand, E., Khosravi, M.R.: Intelligent workload allocation in IoT–fog–cloud architecture towards mobile edge computing. Comput. Commun. **169**, 71–80 (2021)

26. Wang, R., Lu, J.: QoS-aware service discovery and selection management for cloud-edge computing using a hybrid meta-heuristic algorithm in IoT. Wirel. Pers. Commun. 1–14 (2021)

27. Shaheen, Q., Shiraz, M., Hashmi, M.U., Mahmood, D., Zhiyu, Z., Akhtar, R.: A lightweight location-aware fog framework (LAFF) for QoS in internet of things paradigm. Mob. Inf. Syst. **2020**, 1–15 (2020)

28. Vambe, W.T., Sibanda, K.: A fog computing framework for quality of service optimisation in the internet of things (IoT) ecosystem. In: The 2nd International Multidisciplinary Information Technology and Engineering Conference, pp. 1–8 (2020)

29. Springer, T., Linstead, E.: Adaptive QoS-based resource management framework for IoT/edge computing. In: The 9th IEEE Annual Ubiquitous Computing, Electronics & Mobile Communication Conference, pp. 210–217. IEEE (2018)

30. Lai, C.F., Song, D.Y., Hwang, R.H., Lai, Y.X.: A QoS-aware streaming service over fog computing infrastructures. In: Digital Media Industry and Academic Forum, pp. 94–98. IEEE (2016)

31. Chen, Y., Li, Z., Yang, B., Nai, K., Li, K.: A stackelberg game approach to multiple resources allocation and pricing in mobile edge computing. Futur. Gener. Comput. Syst. **108**, 273–287 (2020)

32. Huang, J., Liang, J., Ali, S.: A simulation-based optimization approach for reliability-aware service composition in edge computing. IEEE Access. **8**, 50355–50366 (2020)

33. Ergun, K., Ayoub, R., Mercati, P., Liu, D., Rosing, T.: Energy and QoS-aware dynamic reliability management of IoT edge computing systems. In: The 26th Asia and South Pacific Design Automation Conference, pp. 561–567 (2021)

34. Mordacchini, M., Ferrucci, L., Carlini, E., Kavalionak, H., Coppola, M., Dazzi, P.: Self-organizing energy-minimization placement of QoE-constrained services at the edge. In: Tserpes, K., et al. (eds.) GECON 2021. LNCS, vol. 13072, pp. 133–142. Springer, Cham (2021). https://doi.org/10.1007/978-3-030-92916-9_11

35. Salehie, M., Tahvildari, L.: Self-adaptive software: landscape and research challenges. ACM Trans. Auton. Adapt. Syst. **4**, 1–42 (2009)

36. Krupitzer, C., Roth, F.M., VanSyckel, S., Schiele, G., Becker, C.: A survey on engineering approaches for self-adaptive systems. Pervasive Mob. Comput. **17**, 184–206 (2015)

37. Telecom Dataset. http://sguangwang.com/TelecomDataset.html. Accessed 29 Nov 2021

38. Li, Y., Zhou, A., Ma, X., Wang, S.:Profit-aware edge server placement. IEEE Internet Things J. 1–13 (2021). In press

39. Guo, Y., Wang, S., Zhou, A., Xu, J., Yuan, J., Hsu, C.H.: User allocation-aware edge cloud placement in mobile edge computing. Softw. Pract. Exp. **50**, 489–502 (2020)

40. Wang, S., Guo, Y., Zhang, N., Yang, P., Zhou, A., Shen, X.: Delay-aware microservice coordination in mobile edge computing: a reinforcement learning approach. IEEE Trans. Mob. Comput. **20**, 939–951 (2021)

41. Sonmez, C., Ozgovde, A., Ersoy, C.: EdgeCloudSim: an environment for performance evaluation of edge computing systems. Trans. Emerg. Telecommun. Technol. **29**, 1–17 (2018)

Author Index

Printed in the United States
by Baker & Taylor Publisher Services